M000007045

INCREDIBLE RETREATS

Jim Burns and Mike DeVries

GENERAL
EDITOR

COMPILER

Gospel Light

PUBLISHING STAFF
William T. Greig, Publisher
Dr. Elmer L. Towns, Senior Consulting Publisher
Dr. Gary S. Greig, Senior Consulting Editor
Jill Honodel, Editor
Pam Weston, Assistant Editor
Patti Virtue, Editorial Assistant
Kyle Duncan, Associate Publisher
Bayard Taylor, M.Div., Senior Editor, Theological and Biblical Issues
Barbara LeVan Fisher, Cover Designer
Debi Thayer, Designer

ISBN 0-8307-2403-6
© 1999 by Jim Burns

Contents

Dedication

To my daughter, Mikayla: You are truly a gift from God to your mom and me. I see more clearly what "grace" is all about when I look into your eyes. I love you so very much. May you always know the incredible love and grace that God has for you. I count it a blessing to be your dad.

Thanks and Thanks Again!

To all the students who have participated in camps and retreats as a part of our ministry at Yorba Linda Friends Church: Memories have been treasured and lives have been changed—that's what it's all about.

To my wife, Jamie, and my children, Joshua, Megan and Mikayla: Thanks again for "loaning" Daddy out for a little while for this book. Your love for me is incredible. You are more than I could ever ask for or dream about.

To Megan Jones, my assistant: Thanks for being the left side of my brain and always keeping my life in order. Don't know what I'd do without you!

Contributors

SCOTT CHRISTENSEN
Senior Pastor
Westwood Church
Omaha, Nebraska

MIKE DeVRIES
Pastor of High School Ministries
Yorba Linda Friends Church
Yorba Linda, California

STEVE ERNST
Pastor to Youth
Lutheran Church of the Good
    Shepherd
Torrance, California

JACK HAWKINS
High School Program Director
Forest Home Christian Conference
    Center
Forest Falls, California

BILL REED
Director of Programming
National Institute of Youth Ministry
San Juan Capistrano, California

RUSS VAN NEST
Director, Christian Education and Youth
    Ministries
New Covenant Evangelical Presbyterian
    Church
New Castle, Pennsylvania

Contributors' Submissions

SCOTT CHRISTENSEN
Future Shock!

STEVE ERNST
Experiencing Joy
Faith That Works

JACK HAWKINS
Rock 'n' Roll Weekend

BILL REED
Knowing Who We Serve
Prayer and Service: Putting It All
    Together

RUSS VAN NEST
Love, Sex and Dating: How to Handle
    the Heat!

Introduction

Retreats and camping experiences are such an important part of youth ministry. One parachurch organization I know says that 75 percent of their staff made a significant Christian commitment while at a retreat or camp. Many of us can remember a time away from home when God seemed more real to us, simply because we were away from our normal routines and distractions. As you know, students love all kinds of retreat experiences. There is a sense of excitement and curiosity. Retreats build lifelong memories. In a retreat setting, the atmosphere is casual, fun, relational and frankly, much more spiritually sensitive.

Not long ago, my family was eating a meal in a restaurant near our home. A twenty-something guy walked into the restaurant with a wonderful wife and a rambunctious two-year-old. He looked familiar, but I couldn't get a handle on how I knew him. We watched this lovely family as they were seated near us. When the young man looked up and noticed me, he came right over and introduced himself. Terry told me that when he was fifteen, his first experience with God was at a retreat with our church youth group. Twelve years later, with bright eyes and enthusiasm, he exclaimed to me, "That was the greatest weekend of my life!" As you give students the opportunity to get away from it all to focus on their relationship with God and develop positive peer relationships, you will be offering your students one of the best experiences of their lives.

In this book, we have tried to give you a variety of experiences from some of America's finest youth workers. I'm sure you will find many of these retreat experiences helpful and practical. Like anything else, you will need to adapt the sessions to fit your own group's needs. I hope you'll find this book as helpful as did the youth

workers who have already used the material. Thanks for your commitment to helping students find a closer relationship with God through Christian retreats and camping.

God bless.

Yours in Christ,
Jim Burns, Ph.D.
President,
National Institute of Youth Ministry
San Clemente, California

Retreat Guidelines

I once heard it said that some of the best ministry happens outside the walls of the church. Over the years I've found that to be true, especially in the area of retreats. I can remember being an intern in a junior high ministry and having our junior high pastor remind us that over the approaching weekend retreat, we'd be spending more time with our students than all the hours of Sunday School put together over the entire year. With that thought in mind, our retreat was incredible!

Whether it's a retreat at a camp, in the mountains, on the beach, at a campground, in a hotel or at a lake; whether it's built around a theme, a common goal, a service project or a tour, retreats have a way of changing the lives of everyone involved. The power of retreats is more than just the program. It's the memories, the late-night talks, the lack of sleep and the time spent together. Retreats give us time away from our regular routine, time for God to break through the noise and the busyness and time to see the Spirit of God transform lives and hearts.

So whether you've been on dozens and dozens of retreats or this is your first one ever, our hope is that the retreats found in these pages will help spark your creativity as you venture to see your students' lives transformed by our Lord.

Mike DeVries
Yorba Linda Friends Church
Yorba Linda, California
NIYM

Retreat Ingredients

Schedules

The retreat schedules that are provided in each of the retreat plans are suggested timelines. These may be used as guides in planning your own retreats.

Counselor Meetings

Adult counselors are the key to any retreat's success. Students might not remember the games, the singing or the speaker, but they will always remember their counselors. Counselor meetings are held while students are involved in organized games or activities. Items to discuss during a counselor meeting might include:

- Schedules
- Responsibilities
- Discipline policy
- Appointments with each of their assigned students during the weekend
- Prayer for students

Debriefing Sessions

The debriefing session is a time for you to solidify the growth in each student and prepare them to go home and face the challenges waiting for them. This can be done with the whole group or in smaller groups. Following are some ideas:

- Have students share their most memorable moment at the retreat—let them get as bizarre as they want. Be sure to write all the memories down, so you can share them at retreat reunions later.
- Have students share one thing they learned during the weekend and how they will be different because of it. You may want to have them write this down and give you a copy so that you can challenge students' growth when they return home.
- Pray together for:
  1. Each member's continued growth;
  2. Specific problems students face when they go home;
  3. Group unity.
- Close with a favorite song.
- Assign each student a "contact" at the church—a mentor or small group. It is easier to stay connected with Christ if they stay connected to the church.

- Challenge students to become more involved in youth group activities at home to continue the growth process. Invite them to join in upcoming events or discipleship groups to continue their growth and have account-ability.

Think Tanks

These are suggestions for giving students time to think about, meditate on and apply what they learn in each session. Whatever the time is called, its function is the same: to get students thinking and talking about the messages and to challenge them to apply the lessons learned.

Small Groups

Students tend to assimilate and apply truth through small groups better than they do in large group settings. Because of this, small group times are one of the most important aspects of the retreat.

JAM (Just-A-Moment) Sessions

Using the JAM Session question worksheets, students are divided into small groups where they discuss the questions on the worksheet. If time allows, each small group may share their answers with the whole group.

REACT Sessions

This is another session in which students will join their assigned small groups. The purpose of a REACT Session is to put into action what students have learned from the previous lesson, rather than just discussing it.

Solo Times

Each student needs time alone to meditate on Scripture and the lessons being taught during the weekend. Each solo time should have written guidelines/questions to guide the students during this quiet time of reflection. Students may use this time for Bible study, journaling and prayer.

Fun Times

Hang Time

These are structured activities designed to foster a sense of community between students. The following are suggested resources for crowdbreakers and games that might help you structure Hang Time for the retreat:

> *Games, Crowdbreakers and Community Builders* by Jim Burns and Mark Simone, Gospel Light, 1998
>
> *Up Close and Personal* by Wayne Rice, Youth Specialties, 1989
>
> *Play It!* by Wayne Rice and Mike Yaconelli, Youth Specialties, 1986
>
> *Play It Again!* by Wayne Rice and Mike Yaconelli, Youth Specialties, 1993
>
> *Ideas Library: Games for Youth Groups*, Youth Specialties, 1997
>
> *Ideas Library: Games 2*, Youth Specialties, 1997
>
> *Ideas Library: Crowd Breakers and Mixers for Youth Groups*, Youth Specialties, 1997
>
> *Fresh Ideas: Worship*, Jim Burns, general editor, with Robin Dugall, compiler, Gospel Light, 1999

Campfire Program

The goal here is to give the students a time of worship that leaves them with a sense of God's awesome presence. Students are led in worship, prayer and reflective meditation while gathered around a campfire setting.

Student Leadership Teams

The purpose of student leadership teams is to encourage students to take responsibility during this special time together. Leadership learned while on a retreat can carry over to leadership in the youth group when students return home.

Bon Appetit Team

This team is responsible for loading all food supplies, preparing all meals and cleaning up after the meals. Responsibilities include:
- Review kitchen safety tips.
- Load all food supplies into vehicles.
- Prepare all meals.
- Check ice levels in coolers.
- Prepare drinks.
- Clean up.
- Clean and put away all cooking equipment after the trip.

Transportation Team

This team is responsible for vehicle maintenance and safety. Students are encouraged to help keep all vehicles clean and maintained. Responsibilities include:
- Check vehicle safety: Do all lights work? Are there enough safety belts for all the passengers? Does the horn work?
- Clean windows.
- Clean up trash from vehicles.
- Check vehicle fluids with the driver.
- Check tire pressure.
- Load and unload all luggage and equipment.

Focus Team

This team helps the adult leaders monitor the purpose of the weekend. They also help the adult leaders during the JAM (Just-A-Moment) Sessions or small-group discussion times to encourage fellowship and reflect on the lessons. Responsibilities include:

- Pray as a team before each meeting.
- Learn basic listening skills.
- Review JAM Session/discussion notes.
- Pray together spontaneously throughout the weekend as specific needs arise, such as resolving a conflict or overcoming an obstacle.
- Share Scripture or stories about encouragement.
- Help others stay focused on what the weekend is about.

Recreation Team

This team is responsible for organizing fun times during the retreat. Responsibilities include:

- Organize the recreation time.
- Secure all equipment needed for recreation time.

Equipment Team

This team will help adult leaders collect the equipment that will be used on the trip. They will work with the Transportation Team to insure that the following items are in the vehicles:

- Recreational equipment
- Water supplies
- First-aid kits
- Worship instruments
- Any other supplies specific to the particular retreat

The equipment team will also be responsible for cleaning and putting away equipment after the trip.

Medical and Liability Release

I/We, the undersigned, am/are the parent(s) of _____
(child's name)

(a minor child, ____ years of age), or the person having legal custody pursuant

to authority of _____ or the legal guardian of the
(designate authority, if applicable)

minor child pursuant to an order of _____
(designate authority, if applicable)

and now have, and am/are entitled to the full and complete custody of said minor child.

I/We hereby authorize _____

_____

(church or ministry name and address), its agents, servants, employees, officers and directors, in whose care the minor child has been entrusted by me/us, to consent to any X-ray examination, anesthetic, medical or surgical diagnosis or treatment and hospital care to be rendered to the minor child under the general and special supervision of the California Medicine Practice Act and/or any X-ray examination, anesthetic, dental or surgical diagnosis or treatment and hospital care to be rendered to the minor by a dentist licensed under the provisions of the California Dental Practice Act.

It is understood that this authorization is given in advance of any specific diagnosis, treatment or hospital care being required, but is given to provide authority and power on the part of _____ (church or ministry), its agents, servants, employees, officers and directors, to give specific consent to any and all such diagnosis, treatment or hospital care which a treating physician and/or dentist in the exercise of his/her best judgment may deem advisable in the event of injury to or illness of the minor.

This Authorization shall remain in effect through _____ (date) unless sooner (last day of scheduled activity) revoked by the undersigned in writing, delivered to _____ (church or ministry), its agents, servants, employees, officers and directors from any and all costs and expenses, including but not limited to attorney's fees, reasonable investigative and discovery costs, court costs and all other sums which _____ (church or ministry), its agents, servants, employees, officers and directors may pay or become obligated to pay on account of any, all and every demand for, claim or assertion of liability, or any claim or action founded for, arising or alleged to have arisen out of the activity for which this Authorization is given or the use of real property belonging to _____ (church or ministry), its agents, servants, employees, officers and/or directors, or by any action or omission by the aforesaid minor child.

_____	_____	_____	_____
(Date)	(Mother's Signature)	(Home Phone)	(Work Phone)

_____	_____	_____	_____
(Date)	(Father's Signature)	(Home Phone)	(Work Phone)

_____	_____	_____	_____
(Date)	(Custodian/Guardian's Signature)	(Home Phone)	(Work Phone)

Other emergency contact: _____ Phone _____
Family doctor: _____ Phone _____
Ophthalmologist: _____ Phone _____
Insurance company: _____ Phone _____
Date of last tetanus immunization: _____
Medications/allergies: _____
_____
Will you allow blood transfusions if physician prescribes?_____
Other instructions: _____
_____

Retreat Plans

In each retreat icons point out the following:

 Big Idea—main focus of the session

 Small Group—small group discussion time

 Note—hint or suggestion

 In the Word—Bible study outline

 Fun Times—group activity

 Solo Time—individual reflection/meditation time

Also in each retreat:
The Overview section contains the focus of the weekend and advance preparation pages.

The Plan section outlines the Bible studies and activities for the retreat.

Overview

Rock 'n' Roll Weekend

The Big Idea

Christians and non-Christians can build their lives upon the *Rock*—Jesus Christ.

Key Verse

"Therefore everyone who hears these words of mine and puts them into practice is like a wise man who built his house on the rock." Matthew 7:24

Aims

During this retreat, you will guide students to:
*   Examine the things that we build our lives upon;
*   Discover that Jesus Christ is the only solid foundation: our rock, our refuge and our salvation;
*   Implement a choice to build their lives upon the true rock, our solid foundation—Jesus Christ.

Location

A camping or retreat area with an amusement park, beach or ski resort close by

Time Frame

Friday through Sunday afternoon: If an amusement park or ski retreat is included in the total package, the retreat should start Friday morning with the special activity followed by the official program that evening.

Advance Preparation

Please note: Each group meeting should be aimed at those who don't know Christ or are not familiar with the Church. Therefore, each meeting should include several fun elements. Counselors, musicians and speakers who dress according to the theme of the session will add a special touch as the worship band leads all worship songs.

❑ Organize student leadership teams at least one month before the retreat. Assign an adult leader to oversee each team. See the Retreat Guidelines section on page 11 for suggestions. Suggested teams for this retreat include:
  - Transportation
  - Bon Appetit—Arrange for parents to accompany the group with the primary ministry of supervising this team in meal preparations
  - Equipment
  - Focus
  - Recreation

❑ Set up small groups (five to six students per group) and assign each group an adult leader to facilitate discussions.

❑ Call retreat facility to arrange the use of:
  - The campfire ring, if available
  - A VCR

❑ Ask retreat participants who play a musical instrument to meet and form a worship band for the retreat.

❑ Instruct all retreat staff and band members to dress according to the theme of each session.

❑ Ask adult staff members to prepare a lip-sync performance for the retreat, using plenty of hokey dance moves to enhance the effect.

❑ Prepare a list of trivia questions for the In Search of Elvis Scavenger Hunt, utilizing information about the facility you'll be using. Sample questions:
  - Elvis was heard singing "Heartbreak Hotel" in the one cabin/room with five windows. What is the name/number of the cabin/room?
  - Elvis's best friend's last name is the same as the person the dining room is named after. What's the name?

❑ Announce plans for the Air Band Contest a few weeks before the retreat, giving these general rules:
  - Each group that competes must present a copy of their song and lyrics before the competition. Remind students that they can choose songs from a variety of sources: popular, children's, polka, country, etc.

- Songs must be limited to a maximum of two minutes in length.
- Any inappropriate dance moves during the contest will result in immediate disqualification.

❑ Obtain a copy of the music video *Secret Ambition* by Michael W. Smith.

❑ Record about 15 three- to five-second sound bites from popular 80s songs.

❑ Make photocopies of all reproducible pages:

1. Discussion Starters
   - "Flashback to the Fifties" (p. 42)
   - "The Sixties Scene" (p. 42)
   - "Saturday Night Fever—The Seventies" (p. 43)
2. Solo Time Guidelines and Questions
   - "A Firm or Faulty Foundation?" (p. 44)
   - "Thankful or Thankless?" (p. 45)
3. In Search of Elvis Scavenger Hunt (p. 46)

❑ Purchase Air Band Contest prizes. Inexpensive 40-inch inflatable guitars can be purchased through U. S. Toy Company, (800) 255-6124.

❑ Obtain signed medical and liability release forms from each retreat participant.

❑ Meet with leaders to finalize retreat schedule.

What Leaders Need To Bring

❑ Suggested theme clothes for each meeting (50s, 60s, 70s and 80s rock 'n' roll garb)

❑ Five "Elvis" wigs

❑ Five Hawaiian-style shirts

❑ CDs/tapes of songs of each era to play at meetings

❑ Portable stereo with CD and cassette player

❑ Two microphones for contest props

❑ Four one-minute 50s songs on tape or CD. Some suggestions:
  - "Tutti Frutti" by Little Richard
  - "Hound Dog" by Elvis Presley
  - "Johnny Be Good" by Chuck Berry
  - "Let's Twist Again" by Chubby Checker
  - "Rock Around the Clock" or "Great Balls of Fire" by Jerry Lee Lewis

❑ Tape or CD with several of the following songs included:
  - "The Hokey Pokey"
  - "The Bunny Hop"
  - "The Macarena"
  - "Y.M.C.A."
  - "Willie and the Hand Jive"
  - "Popcorn"
  - "Hound Dog"
  - "Let's Twist Again"
  - "Wipe Out"
  - "Surfin' U.S.A."

❑ Air Band Contest props (optional)

❑ Prizes for crowdbreakers, games and air band contest

❑ Smooth stones, one for each student attending

❑ Several permanent ink felt-tip pens to write on stones

❑ Extra Bibles

❑ 3x5-inch cards

❑ Photocopies of all reproducible pages

❑ Paper and pens/pencils

❑ Michael W. Smith's *Secret Ambition* music video

❑ Buckets of rocks for Rocks of Remembrance Challenge—one rock for each retreat participant

❑ Signed copies of medical and liability release forms

❑

❑

What Students Need to Bring

- ❏ Sleeping bag and pillow
- ❏ Appropriate clothing
- ❏ Theme clothing
- ❏ Toiletries
- ❏ Bible
- ❏ Notebook
- ❏ Pen or pencil
- ❏ Optional: Air Band Contest music, props, costumes
- ❏
- ❏
- ❏

Retreat Schedule

Friday

7:00 P.M.	Dinner
7:45 P.M.	Counselor meeting
8:30 P.M.	Session One: Flashback to the Fifties
10:00 P.M.	Sock Hop
11:15 P.M.	Return to cabins/rooms for discussion
11:45 P.M.	Lights out

Saturday

8:00 A.M.	Breakfast
8:45 A.M.	Solo Time One
9:30 A.M.	Session Two: The Sixties Scene
11:00 A.M.	In Search of Elvis Scavenger Hunt
12:00 P.M.	Lunch
1:00 P.M.	Free time*
5:00 P.M.	Dinner
6:30 P.M.	Session Three: Saturday Night Fever—The Seventies
9:00 P.M.	Air Band Contest
11:00 P.M.	Return to cabins/rooms for discussion
11:30 P.M.	Lights out

Sunday

8:00 A.M.	Breakfast
8:45 A.M.	Solo Time Two
9:30 A.M.	Session Four: The Awesome Eighties
11:00 A.M.	Debriefing Session
12:00 P.M.	Lunch
1:00 P.M.	Retreat ends

*Free Time Suggestions: Too much unstructured free time can lead to mischief or other problems. As a part of free times, be sure to plan some all-group activities, such as hiking, volleyball, softball or any other organized recreation. You can also add creative activities and games: some simply fun activities, some that will build community, or some

that will even teach a point. These activities and games are great for adding a sense of fun and adventure while building some great memories and group camaraderie. See the Retreat Guidelines on page 14 for great resources to aid you in planning activities and games.

The Plan

Rock 'n' Roll Weekend

Session One:
Flashback to the Fifties

Objective

To highlight what people typically build their lives on: relationships, money, popularity, etc., and point out that nothing is really stable unless it's built on the foundation of Christ.

Biblical Basis

Joshua 1:8; Matthew 7:21-29; Luke 6:46-49; John 14:15,21; 1 Peter 2:4-8

Warm-Up: Sing It and Swing It

You'll need:
- Tape player or CD player
- Prop microphone
- The four one-minute prerecorded song segments to play, one for each student

This crowdbreaker is a spontaneous lip sync in which four students are selected to perform one at a time. Each student will hear a different song and must lip-sync it as best they can, including dance moves. The student who gets the best crowd response, lip-syncs most accurately and has the best dance moves is the winner. Remind students they will be disqualified for inappropriate gestures during the song.

Staff Lip Sync
Have your staff perform their choreographed lip sync for the students.

Music/Worship

Have the worship band play a worship song to transition from a wild fever pitch to a more mellow tone so that students will be more receptive to the message.

In the Word: Building Your Life on the Rock

Read Matthew 7:21-29 and Luke 6:46-49.

I. What is your foundation? What is your life built on?
    A. High schoolers base their lives on a lot of different things:
        1. Beauty—Looks
        2. Brains—Achievement, position
        3. Bucks—Possessions
        4. Brawn—Performance
    B. Your foundation is essential. Life is tough and will knock at your foundation.
    C. It takes a sure, solid foundation to make it in life/your Christian walk.

 BIG IDEA When you set your life on a solid foundation, you can stand in the midst of storms.

Reread Matthew 7:24-27.

II. Build a strong foundation.
    A. The cornerstone needs to be Jesus Christ.
        1. Read 1 Peter 2:4-8—Jesus is the cornerstone.
            a. The stone on the bottom corner of a building's foundation from which the other corners of the building are measured
            b. Most important stone in the entire building because from the cornerstone the entire building is set
            c. If your cornerstone is set wrong, your building will be unstable.

Discuss:

What's your cornerstone?
What is the thing that you base your life upon?
Is it solid or faulty?

2. Jesus is the only sure, solid foundation that you can have.
   a. He is trustworthy and sure.
   b. He is faithful and will never change.

B. Follow the building plans.
   1. To build a strong foundation, you need to follow the plans.
   2. Read John 14:15,21—God's love letter to you.
      a. His Word is the building plan for a life built on the foundation of Christ.
      b. Within the pages of His Word, God lays out the building plans.
      c. Put the plans into action using the tools.

Discuss:
Are you picking up the plans?
How are you putting them into action?

C. Get Rid of the S.A.N.D.
   S.A.N.D. is those things that get into our foundations and make them crumble.
   1. S = STORMS
      a. Storms are going to come to test your foundation.
      b. How you handle the storms will determine the strength of your foundation.
   2. A = ATTITUDES
      a. Sometimes our attitudes affect our foundations.
      b. Negative, critical attitudes begin to erode your foundation.
      c. Other people's attitudes may erode your foundation.
   3. N = NOT STANDING FIRM/COMPROMISING
      a. Compromise and temptations not resisted become pebbles that weaken your foundation.
      b. Too many pebbles cause the foundation to crumble in times of stress.
   4. D = DISAPPOINTMENT
      Disappointment can erode our foundations and leave us without the desire to continue.

Discuss:
Which kind of S.A.N.D. is weakening your foundation?

D. Pick up your tools daily.

1. Building a foundation takes time—it's a life-long process.
   a. Celebrate the small victories in your life as you build your foundation.
   b. Don't expect perfection overnight.
   c. God is not looking for perfection, but progression!
   d. Take the time and effort to build upon your foundation daily.
2. Read Joshua 1:8—Do something about what you've heard tonight!
   a. Decide to allow Jesus to be your foundation.
   b. Pick up the building plans more often and use them.
   c. Make a conscious decision to get rid of S.A.N.D.
   d. Choose to build on your foundation every day.
III. Conclusion
This weekend you will learn how you can build your life on a rock that is so stable, it can never be shaken!

Small-Group Discussion

Give each student a copy of the discussion sheet "Flashback to the Fifties" and a pen or pencil. Have students discuss the questions within their small groups and, if time permits, bring the whole group together to recap and discuss the small-group discoveries.

THROUGH THE AGES SOCK HOP

This activity has a 50s feel but includes songs from other eras as well. Rather than putting on a CD and letting kids have at it, the sock hop is designed to get the maximum number of students involved. Most dances can be done without a partner. Some specific suggestions for extra fun:

- Elvis Dance-Off : Select five students to wear Elvis wigs and do their best Elvis impersonation one at a time, each to a different song.
- "Wipe Out" Drum Solo: Have five students come to the front and give them each two unsharpened pencils and a trash can or chair to drum on.
- "Surfin' U.S.A.": Give five students each a Hawaiian shirt to wear and ask them to come to the front and lead the other students in the Swim.

SOLO TIME ONE:
A FIRM OR FAULTY FOUNDATION?

Give each student a copy of the handout, "A Firm or Faulty Foundation?" and a pen or pencil. Instruct them to spend time alone and, using their Bibles, a notebook and the handout, meditate on what they've learned.

Session Two:
The Sixties Scene

Have the staff dress in 60s style—surfer duds, peace signs, tie dye, Beatles, Beach Boys, etc.—and play 60s music as students enter.

Objective

To help students see that one of the greatest benefits of living your life on the Rock is having a place of refuge in times of trouble. He is the one person you can always take refuge in.

Biblical Basis

2 Samuel 22:1-8; Matthew 14:22-33

Warm-Up: Sixties Song Burst

- Divide the whole group into two fairly even teams.
- Set up two microphones on each side of the front of the room, one for each team.
- Play a popular 60s song. Use songs that are fairly well known i.e., from the Beatles, Beach Boys, Monkees, etc. Stop each song in mid-sentence.
- The first team to have a student run to the microphone and finish singing the sentence gets one point. The team with the most points wins.

Music/Worship

Have the worship band play one or two worship songs as a transition to the message.

In THE WORD

In the Word: The Rock of Refuge

Read 2 Samuel 22:1-8.

I. All of us go through tough times in our lives—times of loneliness or other storms in our lives—when God seems miles away, way out of reach.

   A. "Storms of Life" such as graduation, school, home, family, illness—whether good or bad events—add to the stress of life.

   B. "Storms of Doubt" that cause us to ask, If God is God, then why? Why divorce? Why is my home a battlefield? Why doesn't He answer my prayers?

Discuss:

What do you hold on to?

What's your anchor in the midst of the storm?

   C. Christianity isn't just for getting into heaven—or fire insurance—it impacts your life in the here and now!

   D. God was the Rock of refuge for David in the midst of his storms (see 2 Samuel 22:3).

      1. He's closer than you've ever dreamed. Even when you can't see Him, He's still there!

      2. When you can't go on, He'll carry you through the storms.

BIG IDEA

Jesus is in the middle of your storm with you. He's right there!

Read Matthew 14:22-33.

II. The view from the boat

   A. Jesus sent the disciples into the storm (vv. 22-24).

      1. Jesus knew about the storm and willingly sent the disciples into the middle of it.

      2. Jesus allows us to go through the storms in our lives.

      3. He knows what's going on in your life today.

   B. Jesus comes to them in the storm (vv. 25,26).

      1. Jesus sends them out at about 6:00 P.M. and the storm hits!

      2. The disciples' reactions are the same as ours in times of turmoil.

         a. Where is Jesus when you need Him? Has He forgotten us? Doesn't He care about what's going on?

b. Fourth watch comes and so does Jesus—3:00 A.M. to 6:00 A.M.

c. Imagine being between verse 24 and verse 25!

3. Jesus knows about your storms and He cares. He won't leave you alone in the midst of your storms.

C. Jesus encourages them in the storm (v. 27).

1. "Take courage." I know all about the storm.

2. "It is I." Remember who I am, remember what I just did— fed the 5,000.

3. "Don't be afraid." I can do all things and will save even you.

4. Jesus longs to say the same things to you this morning in the midst of your storm.

D. Jesus is with them in the storm (vv. 28-31).

1. Peter saw Jesus, called to Him and walked on the water.

2. When Peter took his focus off the Lord of the circumstances and focused on the circumstances themselves, he began to sink!

3. Where is your focus? In the midst of the storm, what do you see—the storm or the Master of the waves, our Rock of refuge?

4. Jesus was only an arm's length away from Peter. He's that close to you right now. Can you see Him?

E. Jesus is the Lord of the storm (vv. 32,33).

1. Jesus was in control of the storm. He climbed back in the boat and the storm calmed down.

2. Jesus is the Lord of your storms. He is the One who is in control.

3. He can take a bad situation/circumstance and use it for good.

4. Reach out to Him. He will be your Anchor in the midst of the waves and wind of the storm. He will be your Rock of refuge!

Small-Group Discussion

Give each student a copy of the discussion sheet "The Sixties Scene" and a pen or pencil. Have students discuss the questions within their small groups and, if time permits, rejoin as a large group to recap and discuss the small-group discoveries.

SMALL GROUP.

In Search of Elvis Scavenger Hunt

Divide students into groups of four or five and give each team a copy of the "In Search of Elvis Scavenger Hunt" sheet and a pencil. Read the following statement aloud:

> **Elvis has recently been spotted in the area. Authorities are looking for him and have offered a reward for any information regarding his whereabouts. Your job is to collect as much information about Elvis as possible. The group to gather the most information in the next 45 minutes is the winner.**

After the students return, collect each team's answer sheet and tell them you will announce a winner tonight. Give each team one point for each correct answer. Arrange a surprise appearance by a staff person dressed as Elvis to present the winning team their prize during Session 3 Warm-Up time.

Session Three: Saturday Night Fever—The Seventies

Pull out the polyester and gold chains and have each staff member dress for the disco era. Have some Bee Gees or other disco music playing as students enter.

You'll need a VCR for this session to play the Michael W. Smith videotape.

Objective

To help students gain an understanding of the importance of building their lives on the Rock with the foremost stone for their lives' foundation being salvation; to help students understand the power and the meaning of the Crucifixion and the Resurrection.

Biblical Basis

Matthew 27:26-50; John 3:16,17; 19:30; Romans 3:21-25; 5:1,6-8; 6:23; 1 Peter 1:18,19; 2:21-25; 3:18

Warm-Up: Y.M.C.A. Dance Fever

Get staff members on the stage and have them lead the entire group in the hand motions of "Y.M.C.A."

Seventies Counselor Sing-Off

You'll need:
- A personal tape or CD player with headphones
- Four different 70s tunes to play on the tape or CD player

Select four counselors from the crowd and tell them you are having a sing-off. Then have the first counselor put on the headphones and sing along with the music. Be sure the volume is turned up loud enough so they can't hear themselves sing—which in most cases makes the counselors tone-deaf. The results are hysterical.

Have each of the counselors perform a different song; then have students vote for the best one.

Entrance of Elvis

Play an Elvis song as one of your staff members dressed as Elvis makes his/her way to the stage to present prizes to the winning team of the "In Search of Elvis Scavenger Hunt."

Music/Worship

Have the worship band play one or two worship songs as a transition to the message.

In The Word: The Rock of Salvation

Most rock 'n' roll musicians are trying to give a message through their lyrics. Read aloud the following quotes from rock 'n' roll stars to help your students get an idea of the type of person they're allowing themselves to be influenced by when they listen to music (quotes taken from *Youth Worker Update* by Youth Specialties).

The first time I smoked pot, I was with my dad, and to me, it just seemed like I'd landed in this magical kingdom

where anything was possible. I got stoned, and my father had a girl over at the house, and she didn't have her shirt on. I said to myself, *You know, how lucky could a boy be?* At the time I thought I was the luckiest kid on the block (Red Hot Chili Peppers' Anthony Kiedis, in a *Rolling Stone* interview).

Well, for the first time, I'm feeling free. I love feeling deeply sexual and don't mind letting the world know (Janet Jackson, in a *Rolling Stone* interview).

I'd like to give a message to the youth of America. We will continue to abuse our position and [mess] up the mainstream (U2's Bono in his acceptance speech at the Grammys, *San Diego Union Tribune*, March 2, 1994).

Our music is either the result of brain damage caused by huffing or it's the musical equivalent of huffing gas. We don't encourage gas huffing. Just huff up those punk rock fumes, and be cool, stay in school (Joe Newton, drummer for the band Gas Huffer, in a *Rolling Stone* interview).

I think everybody takes drugs for the same reason. People do it to escape. A lot of performers are very insecure people and part of the whole reason why we want fame is that we want to be loved. What you find is that when you reach that peak where you're supposed to be satisfied, you're feeling just as empty because nothing outside of yourself can make you feel whole (pop singer Boy George in a *Rolling Stone* interview).

I. You need a Savior!
   A. Rock and roll musicians have a message, but at the heart of most rock music you find a message that is shallow, self-serving and hollow.
   B. You can think that you have it all, but without a relationship with Jesus Christ, it's all empty.

Explain: **Tonight I want to paint a portrait of what Jesus did for you and me.**

He saw your face; He knew your name! | **BIG IDEA**

Show the video *Secret Ambition* by Michael W. Smith.

II. The Scene: The view from the Cross
  A. Read Matthew 27:26-50 to see what Jesus really went through.
    1. Flogging with a whip, the beating
    2. The humiliation of the scarlet robe: the mocking, spitting, stripping, etc.
    3. Crown of thorns: two-inch thorns, pushed into His head
    4. Carrying the 200-pound cross the length of two football fields
    5. Crucifixion: the nails, the cross, death by suffocation
  B. Why did Jesus go to the Cross?
    1. You need a Savior.
      a. The price needed to be paid (see Romans 6:23).
      b. You needed a way back to God (see 1 Peter 3:18).
    2. He couldn't bear to live without you.
      a. He couldn't stand the thought that you would be separated from Him for all eternity.
      b. Because of His love for you, He went to the Cross to make a way for you to have a relationship with Him.
  C. What happened for you on the Cross?
    1. You were justified.
      a. It means "just-as-if-I'd-never-sinned" (see Romans 3:22-24).
      b. You were given complete forgiveness.
      c. The slate was wiped clean because of His blood that was shed.
      d. God no longer sees your sin. He sees Jesus!
    2. You were atoned for/redeemed.
      a. The price was paid in full (see 1 Peter 1:18,19).
      b. What should have happened to you (death) happened to Jesus instead.
      c. He took your place on the Cross.
III. Challenge: Jesus went to the Cross to "bridge the gap" so you could have a way back to God!
IV. Decision time: To close your message time, give students an opportunity to make a decision for Jesus Christ, whether a first-time decision or a recommitment. Be sure to clearly explain what

Jesus did for us on the Cross and how we can enter into a relationship with Him. Lead students in a time of prayer for their commitment to Christ.

A. Encourage students to raise a hand, stand in place or come forward to take a stand for their commitment to Christ.

B. Have students around those who are making their commitment lay hands on them and pray for them after their prayer of commitment.

C. Have students write down their commitment to Christ on a 3x5-inch card. You may want them to write it on two cards and give one to you for follow-up.

Small-Group Discussion

Give each student a copy of the discussion sheet "Saturday Night Fever—The Seventies" and a pen or pencil. Have students discuss the questions within their small groups and, if time permits, bring the whole group together to recap and discuss the small-group discoveries.

AIR BAND CONTEST

Each band must arrive a half hour before the beginning of the contest to check in and get their act ready. Groups will take turns trying to lip-sync and "play" their song while it's being played over the sound system.

- Have an emcee welcome the crowd and explain the event.
- Allow each performing group one minute to set up their props.
- After each group has performed, have a panel of three judges give a 1 to 10 score based on creativity, lip sync, dance moves and crowd response.
- After all bands have performed, announce the winner and have them come to the stage for their prize.

SOLO TIME TWO:
THANKFUL OR THANKLESS?

Give each student a copy of the Solo Time handout "Thankful or Thankless?" (p. 45) and a pen or pencil. Instruct them to spend time alone and, using their Bibles, a notebook and the handout, meditate on what they've learned.

Session Four:
The Awesome Eighties

Objective

To guide students in remembering and reflecting on all that God has done for them and taking steps to renew their love for Him.

Biblical Basis

Joshua 4:1-7

Warm-Up: 80s Name That Tune

Play the 15 prerecorded three- to five-second sound bites from popular 80s songs and have students take turns naming the tunes. If the student gets it right, he or she wins a prize.

Music/Worship

Have the worship band play one or two worship songs as a transition to the message.

In the Word: The Rock of Remembrance

Read Joshua 4:1-7. Explain the scenario: **The rocks were chosen to be a remembrance, one that lasted a lifetime and would be something that the Israelites could share with their children about how God had met their needs, provided for them and cared for them in the wilderness.**

This weekend we've been remembering rock n' roll through the ages and it's amazing how much we remember (cite the trivia game). **Yet how much do we remember about all the great things God has done for us? Sometimes I think we remember rock 'n' roll lyrics from 10 years ago better than we remember the blessings that God has given us this last year.**

Discuss:

What would your rock of remembrance be this morning from this weekend/the past year?

1. Remember.

    A. What God has done for us. He is...

       1. Our solid Rock—He is the solid foundation who we can build our lives upon.

       2. Our Rock of refuge—He is with us in the storms, only an arm's length away.

       3. The Rock of our salvation—He is the only one who we find salvation in.

    B. What God has done in your life the past year.

  II. Reflect.

    A. You need to take time alone to reflect on all that God has done for you. He has done all this because...

       1. He created you.

       2. He loves you.

       3. He cares for you.

       4. He couldn't stand to live without you.

Have you ever taken the time to just say thank you to God for all the incredible things He has done for you?

    B. Take time regularly to reflect on God's goodness, mercy, grace and all the things He has done for you. It'll make you a person of thankfulness!

  III. Renew.

    A. After we've remembered and reflected, we can't help but renew our love for Him.

    B. When we see God for who He is and what He's done for us, it should drive us to our knees in thankfulness.

Explain: **This morning, we want to give you an opportunity to remember, reflect and renew before we leave to go home.**

Challenge: Rocks of Remembrance

- Invite the students to come forward and take a rock from one of the buckets. Remind them that as they look back at that rock, they can remember what God did in their lives this weekend.

- **Option:** Have students use permanent felt-tip pens to write the date of the retreat and a reference verse or "Jesus is my Rock" on their rocks.

- Close with a time of reflection and worship.

Debriefing Session

- Have a time for students to reflect on the weekend and what they learned. This can be done just before you leave the retreat or when you return home. If you wait to debrief upon your return, do it before students leave for their homes.
- See page 12 in the Retreat Guidelines section for debriefing session ideas.

Discussion Starters

Session One: Flashback to the Fifties

1. What is one thing that you could do this weekend to strengthen the foundation of your spiritual life?

2. Describe a time in your life when you started to set your spiritual foundation.

3. What are some of the foundation crumblers in your life (S.A.N.D.)?

4. Who in our youth group or your family helps you strengthen your foundation?

Discussion Starters

Session Two: The Sixties Scene

1. What are some of the storms in your life right now?

2. How do you deal with the storms?

   How are you dealing with the current storm?

3. How does the fact that Jesus is only an arm's length away impact you in the midst of your storm?

4. When you go home from this retreat, what do you need to do, change, etc. to deal with your storm?

Discussion Starters

Session Three: Saturday Night Fever—The Seventies

1. Imagine you are at the Crucifixion. You're a follower of Jesus and you're standing at the edge of the crowd. What would you be thinking and feeling as you watch all this take place?

2. Read John 19:30. Jesus' last words before He died were "It is finished." What did Jesus accomplish when He died on the Cross?

3. Read 1 Peter 2:21-25. What do these verses say about what Jesus did for you?

   How does Christ's suffering on the Cross help you understand His love for you?

4. How should we respond to what Jesus did for us on the Cross? How will you respond to Jesus' offer of forgiveness and salvation?

5. What does the following statement mean to you?
   When Jesus was on the Cross, He saw your face and He knew your name.

6. Look at the following verses and explore why Jesus died for each and every one of us:

   John 3:16,17

   Romans 3:21-25

   Romans 5:1

   Romans 5:6-8

   1 Peter 3:18

Solo Time One:

A Firm or Faulty Foundation?

1. Take a moment to evaluate how you spend your time on a weekly basis. Using a typical school week, how much time, in hours, do you spend on the following activities each week?

    _____ Watching TV   _____ Reading   _____ Extracurricular activities
    _____ Working   _____ Homework   _____ Reading the Bible
    _____ Phone calls   _____ At church   _____ Playing video games
    _____ Getting ready   _____ Eating   _____ Hanging with friends
    _____ Sleeping   _____ Praying   _____ Brushing teeth

2. Circle the three activities you spend most of your time on each week. Draw a square around the three activities you spend the least amount of time on.

3. Read Matthew 6:19-21. According to your list, what do you treasure and where is your heart—what do you spend the most time on?

4. What did this list show you about what you *are* building your life on and what you're *not* building it on?

5. Review Matthew 7:21-29. What are the benefits of building your life on the Rock?

6. One of the benefits of building your life on the Rock is that God can become your refuge in times of trouble. Read 2 Samuel 22:1-7 and list all the words that refer to God as a refuge.

7. What is one difficulty you are currently going through?

8. How can it benefit you to have God as your foundation and refuge as you go through this time?

Solo Time Two:

Thankful or Thankless?

If we are honest with ourselves we would have to admit it's easier to complain than to be thankful, easier to spread gossip than glory. We tune into the news to hear about bombings and murder, rather than focus on the good around us. Our God has given us so much, yet it's easier to focus on what we don't have and on the negativity around us.

1. What are the top ten things high school students complain about?

2. What spreads faster around your school: good juicy gossip or good news?

3. What type of stories do you hear about during the first five minutes of a TV newscast?

4. Read the following verses and write what God tells us about being thankful.

    Psalm 42:4

    Psalm 69:30

    Psalm 100:4

    Ephesians 5:4

    Philippians 4:6

5. On the back of this sheet, make a top-ten list of the things you have to be thankful to God for.

In Search of Elvis Scavenger Hunt

1. One person on the grounds has a tape player with 10 clips from Elvis songs. Find him/her and identify as many songs as you can. Each is worth one point.

2. One person on the grounds is auditioning acts to become the next Elvis. Find the person with the video camera and sing three lines of your favorite Elvis song.

3.

4.

5.

6.

Overview

Future Shock!

The Big Idea

Although the future is an uncertain place, we can know a few things for certain. Jesus is coming back someday and if we know Jesus as Savior, there is a place reserved for us in heaven. Those wonderful facts can help us deal with the tough parts of life and rejoice in the joys of life.

Key Verses

"They asked him, 'Lord, are you at this time going to restore the kingdom to Israel?' He said to them: 'It is not for you to know the times or dates the Father has set by his own authority.'" Acts 1:6,7

"'Men of Galilee,' they said, 'why do you stand here looking into the sky? This same Jesus, who has been taken from you into heaven, will come back in the same way you have seen him go into heaven.'" Acts 1:11

Aims

During this retreat, you will guide students to:
- Examine fears about the future and the trustworthiness of God;
- Discover what the Bible says about the future and learn denominational perspectives of the biblical message;
- Implement action steps to live life as if Jesus were to return tomorrow.

Location

This retreat can take place at any camping area or retreat facility within 60 to 90 minutes from your church. For added effect, you could do this retreat in a paradise-type environment, to help your students think of the worldly view of heaven.

Time Frame

Saturday morning through Sunday morning

Advance Preparation

❏ Assign student leadership teams.
- Transportation
- Bon Appetit
- Equipment
- Focus

❏ Set up small REACT Groups (five to six students per group) and assign each group an adult leader to facilitate discussions.

❏ Arrange for the retreat group to meet at your church the morning of the retreat for fellowship and breakfast.
- Ask for church volunteers to help with the food preparation and cleanup.

❏ Create a poster with the title "Hangin' onto Heaven" written at the top (see p. 64).

❏ Using gray construction paper, cut out enough rock shapes for each student to have three.

❏ Obtain the following videos:
- *Raiders of the Lost Ark,* cued to the climactic scene where the Ark is opened
- An old, campy black-and-white science fiction movie (*Attack of the Killer Tomatoes,* for instance) cued to the scene that sets the plot for the movie

Reminder: It is illegal to *rent* a video at the video store and show it to your youth group without first having purchased a license to do so. A blanket movie license can be bought that will allow you to show virtually any movie to your youth group for one year by calling the Motion Picture Licensing Corporation at 1-800-462-8855.

❏ Fast-forward through *Raiders of the Lost Ark* to the final scene where the Ark of the Covenant is opened.

❏ Preview the second video and note a five- to eight-minute section in which the scenario of the movie is set.

❏ Arrange the use of a VCR and TV at the retreat facility (if one is not available, make arrangements to bring a portable TV and VCR).

❏ Photocopy the reproducible student page "What About You in 10, 20, 30 Years?" (p. 65).

❏ Obtain signed medical and liability release forms from each retreat participant.

❏ Meet with leaders to finalize retreat schedule.

What Leaders Need to Bring

- ❏ 3x5-inch index cards
- ❏ Paper and pens/pencils
- ❏ Felt-tip pens
- ❏ Large sheets of newsprint, three for each small group
- ❏ Several sheets of poster board, one for each small group
- ❏ Portable TV and VCR (if none available at retreat facility)
- ❏ Gray construction paper "rocks"
- ❏ Photocopies of student pages
- ❏ Signed copies of medical and liability release forms
- ❏
- ❏
- ❏

What Students Need to Bring

- ❏ Sleeping bag and pillow
- ❏ Toiletries
- ❏ Appetite and smiles
- ❏ Extra spending money
- ❏ Bible
- ❏ Notebook
- ❏ Pen or pencil
- ❏
- ❏
- ❏

Retreat Schedule

Saturday

7:30 A.M.	Arrive at church for breakfast together, perhaps sponsored by some of the parents or by the student leadership group. Have a meal to kick off your weekend together.
8:00-9:30 A.M.	Travel to retreat center
9:30-9:45 A.M.	Settle in
9:45-11:00 A.M.	Session One: Future Fears
11:00-11:45 A.M.	REACT Session One
12:00-1:00 P.M.	Lunch
1:00-1:15 P.M.	Session Two: Future Returns
1:15-2:00 P.M.	REACT Session Two
1:45-5:30 P.M.	Free time*
5:30-6:30 P.M.	Dinner
6:30-7:45 P.M.	Session Three: A Futuristic Lifestyle
7:45-8:30 P.M.	REACT Session Three
8:30-9:30 P.M.	Free time*
9:30-11:00 P.M.	Movie**
11:15 P.M.	Return to rooms
11:30 P.M.	Lights out

Sunday

8:00-8:30 A.M.	Breakfast
8:30-8:50 A.M.	Quiet time
8:50-9:30 A.M.	Free time*
9:30-11:00 A.M.	Worship Service: Being Heavenly Minded
11:00-11:30 A.M.	Pack it up/clear it out
11:30 A.M.	Leave for home

Free Time Suggestions: Too much unstructured free time can lead to mischief or other problems. As a part of free times, be sure to plan some all-group activities, such as hiking, volleyball, softball or any other organized recreation. You can also add some creative activities and games: some that are simply fun activities, some that will build community, or some that will even teach a point. These activities and games are great for adding a sense of fun and adventure while building some

great memories and group camaraderie. See the Retreat Guidelines section on page 14 for great resources to aid you in planning activities and games.

**Obtain an old campy science fiction movie such as *Attack of the Killer Tomatoes* or something similar.

The Plan

Future Shock!

Session One:
Future Fears

Objective

Students will learn that when they have fears about their future on Earth and after they die, they can trust God with their fears and rely on His promises.

Biblical Basis

Genesis 6:9—8:11; 12:1-10; 13:1,2; 39; Judges 4:1-16; Ecclesiastes 8:7,8; Matthew 6:25-34; Luke 1:26-45; 2:1-16; Romans 10:9,10; Philippians 3:17—4:1; Hebrews 11:7-9; James 4:13-15; 1 John 5:11,12

Warm-Up: The Vast Unknown

- If you have not done so before the retreat, divide students into REACT Groups of five to six per group according to the students' responses to the following question: Who are you most like? (Make sure the groups are divided as evenly as possible.)

  Mr. Spock
  Captain Kirk
  Han Solo
  Princess Leia
  R2D2
  Other future-type characters

  Add as many groups as you need so that you will have enough groups.
- The group names then become the names of their characters. So you will have the Spocks, the R2D2s, etc.

- **Option:** Assign the names to the groups ahead of time if you think the groups will be numerically out of balance.

Team Effort: Future Expectations

- Ask: **Everyone thinks about the future. What do you expect in the future?**
- After a few minutes of discussion, give each student a copy of the "What About You in 10, 20, 30 Years?" handout (p. 65) and a pen or pencil. Allow about 10 minutes for students to complete handouts, then have them join their REACT Groups to share their answers.
- Bring the whole group back together and discuss the following questions:
    1. **What was the most interesting prediction in your group?**
    2. **What was the most surprising prediction?**
    3. **What was the most hopeful prediction?**
    4. **What fears were expressed about the future?**
- Explain: **Everyone has some fears about the future.** Share a few future fears that you have (i.e., the safety of your family, your parents' health problems, etc.). Try to be appropriately vulnerable.

In the Word: The Truth About the Future

I. Three truths about the future
   A. Truth One: We can't know what is going to happen.
      1. Ecclesiastes 8:7,8 tells us that none of us can know what will happen in the future, so that we will not avoid it or change it.
      2. James 4:13-15 warns that even though we might make plans for the future only God knows what our future holds.
   B. Truth Two: We can trust God with our future.
      1. Give each group one of the following Bible characters and Scripture references. Instruct them to read the story and act it out briefly and without words as you read the passage for the rest of the group.
      2. Have each group explain how and why each character trusted God with his or her future.
         a. Abraham: Genesis 12:1-10; 13:1,2; Hebrews 11:8,9
         b. Noah: Genesis 6:9—8:11; Hebrews 11:7

c. Joseph: Genesis 39
d. Deborah: Judges 4:1-16
e. Mary: Luke 1:26-45; 2:1-16

 BIG IDEA God proved Himself trustworthy over and over in the Bible. We can trust Him with our futures, too!

C. Truth Three: Heaven awaits all who believe.
Read the following passages and make the following observations:
1. Romans 10:9,10
   a. The only way to get to heaven is through Jesus Christ.
   b. Those who confess Him as Lord are assured of going to heaven.
2. First John 5:11,12
   a. There is life in the Son—only in Him.
   b. If you do not have the Son, you do not have eternal life, or heaven!
3. Philippians 3:17—4:1
   a. As Christians, our citizenship is in heaven. What does that mean?
   b. We are called to eagerly await the return of the Savior which means our lives need to be in order, living every day as He would desire us to live.
II. Conclusion: Future fears
A. No matter who you talk to or what you do, you can't know what is going to happen in your future.
B. God proved Himself trustworthy over and over in the Bible. We can trust Him with our futures, too!
C. The only thing you can know for sure about your future is that if you are a believer in Jesus Christ, you are headed for heaven. But heaven only has rooms reserved for those who have personal relationships with Jesus. Is that you? Is your place in heaven reserved for you?

REACT
SESSION ONE

Future Fantasy Four

- Give each student a 3x5-inch index card and a pen or pencil.
- Have each student write at the top of the card the vocation he or she would like to pursue in the next five or ten years; then have him or her write three clues about that vocation. The vocations the students choose should be serious, but their clues can be funny or serious. Ask them to keep their future vocations and the clues secret.
- Collect the completed cards and shuffle them thoroughly.
- Next, give each student a blank sheet of paper. Instruct students to number down the paper from one to the number of youths attending the meeting.
- While students are numbering their papers, number the index cards you've collected from them.
- When the papers and cards are ready, read aloud the *number* of the vocation and the clues on the first card, asking everyone to write their guess about what the vocation is and who wrote the clues. Remind them not to comment aloud on any of the cards or on their own responses.
- After you've read through all the clue cards, repeat any as needed for clarification.
- Next, go through the cards again and ask the person who wrote each one to reveal him- or herself. The results will be fun and surprising.
- Have students join their assigned REACT groups and discuss the following questions:
  1. What do teenagers fear most about the future?
  2. What do you fear most about the future?
  3. Read Matthew 6:25-34. Does God want you to worry about the future? Why or why not?
  4. What hope does God offer for your future?
- Close with a prayer that students' futures will be centered on God and His Word.

Session Two: Future Returns

Objective

Students will explore what the Bible says about the end times and discover that we may not know exactly when and how Jesus is coming back, but we do know for certain that He *is* coming back!

Biblical Basis

Matthew 24:1-44; Luke 21:7-31; Acts 1:1-12; 1 Thessalonians 4:13-18; Hebrews 10:24,25; 2 Peter 3:1-14; Jude 14-24

Warm-Up: The Ending Has Not Been Written

From the science fiction video that you selected before the retreat, show the clip that sets the scene. Stop the film just as the students are getting into it. Divide the students into their small groups and instruct them to write an ending for the movie. Have groups share their endings.

Tell students you'll all watch the whole movie later this evening!

In the Word: Future Returns

Explain: **The story of Jesus is not over—because we do not know the ending.**
Read Acts 1:1-12.
 I. There are a lot of things people think about when it comes to the end of the world.
   A. Imagine the climactic end of the Book.
      Cue up the climactic scene in *Raiders of the Lost Ark* where the Ark of the Covenant is opened. Before showing the video clip, explain that what the group is about to see is what a lot of people think will happen at the end of the world. Show the clip.[1]
   B. Discuss the following:

1. When you think about the end of the world, what do you think of?
2. What does the devil want us to think about the end of this world?
3. What does the Bible have to say about the end of the world?

II. What does the Bible actually say?

A. Divide students into five groups. Give each group one of the following passages of Scripture and ask them to write a summary of what their assigned scripture says about the end times.

B. Have the small groups share their summaries.
   1. Matthew 24:1-44
   2. Luke 21:7-31
   3. 1 Thessalonians 4:13-18
   4. 2 Peter 3:1-14
   5. Jude 1:14-24

Explain: **It is important to listen to what the Bible actually says about the future instead of what you might want it to say.** Teach students what your church/denomination believes about the general eschatological (end-time) message of the Scripture, but be careful not to go beyond what God's Word actually says.

III. What are your questions?

Give students 3x5-inch cards and pens or pencils. Have each student write one or two questions that he or she has about the end times. Collect the cards. Read through them and discuss with the whole group.

IV. Conclusion

Ask: **If Jesus were to pull into your driveway tomorrow, would He be pleased with your life?**

A. Jesus is coming back. We don't know when.

B. Think about what you would change if you knew for certain that Jesus was going to return tomorrow.

C. God has given us only faint glimpses into the future to encourage us to live as disciples of Jesus in the present, realizing that we must live as though He might return at any moment. Read Hebrews 10:24,25.

REACT
SESSION TWO

Future World

Use this activity and discussion to alert students to the effect today's activities and preparations have on their futures, and how the Church can help in preparing them for the future.

- Have students join their assigned REACT Group. Give each group three large sheets of newsprint paper and some felt-tip pens.
- Read the following questions one at a time (or write them on the board or an overhead transparency), giving students a few minutes to suggest and discuss answers within their small groups.
  1. List some characteristics of the world as you think it will be in ten years.
  2. List some characteristics of the kind of person who will best be able to deal with the world as it will exist ten years from now.
  3. List five goals the Church should adopt in order to prepare people for living in the world of the future.
- Have each group record its ideas on the large sheets of paper, and then report their answers back to the entire group. Have a reporting time after each question is discussed.
- After all their answers have been presented and discussed, ask them what they are doing now to prepare themselves spiritually for the future. In responding to the last question, many will realize that the Church is already attempting to prepare young people for the future, but they (the students) aren't taking advantage of all the opportunities offered. Youth workers may also discover some student needs that are presently being overlooked.

Session Three:
A Futuristic Lifestyle

 Session Three is adapted from *The Word on the New Testament* by Mike DeVries.[2]

Objective

Students will examine the fact that since Jesus is coming back, we have to commit our lives to serving Christ by serving others.

Biblical Basis

Mark 13:35-37; Luke 10:29-37; 1 Corinthians 13:12; 1 Thessalonians 5:1-6; 2 Peter 3:10-13; 1 John 3:2,3; Revelation 3:2,3; 4:1-8; 21:1-7; 22:7,12,20

Team Effort: Time Is Ticking

- Explain: **If we believe that Jesus is going to come back, we need to live our lives as if He were coming back any minute.** Read Hebrews 10:24,25.
- Divide students into groups of four or five.
- Give each group a set of 3x5-inch cards with one of the following written on a separate card in each set:

    1 hour   1 week   1 month   1 year   10 years

- Give each small group a set of the five cards. Have the group members distribute the cards face down, one to each group member. Ask students to consider the time frame on their cards as they answer the following question:
    How would you feel and what would you do if the world was going to end at the time written on your card?
- After giving the small groups time to share their answers, bring the whole group back together and have a few people share their reactions. Then discuss the following questions:
    1. **What were your feelings and reactions to the time given you?**
    2. **How would your life be different because of your time frame?**
    3. **What happened as the time got shorter and shorter?**
    4. **What are some lessons from this activity that can be applied to our lives today?**

In the Word: Revelation—The Hope, Encouragement and Call

The Call of Christ
Explain: **The book of Revelation is a book of hope, encouragement, judgment, and a call to all Christians. Within the pages are the**

scenes for the end of the world, the triumph of God over Satan, the final judgment of the world and the incredible description of what heaven will be like. As Christians, the book is written to be an encouragement, as well as a call to readiness. Throughout the pages of Revelation, God is calling us to stand firm, be encouraged and be ready for the return of Christ.

I. Be encouraged.
  A. What hope or promise is found in the following passages?
    1. 1 Corinthians 13:12
    2. 1 John 3:2,3
    3. Revelation 21:1-7
  B. What would it be like to see God face-to-face? Read Revelation 4:1-8 for the description. What would you say to Him?
  C. What does it mean to know Him even as He knows us?
  D. As you read Revelation 21:1-7, which of the following words best describes your feeling?

Thankful	Relieved
Valuable	Awe-filled
Renewed	Amazed
Unworthy	Complete
Other _____	

  E. How do these promises impact your life in the here and now?
II. Be ready.
  A. What encouragement are we given in the following passages?
    1. Mark 13:35-37
    2. 1 Thessalonians 5:1-6
    3. 2 Peter 3:10-13
    4. Revelation 3:2,3
    5. Revelation 22:7,12,20
  B. What does it mean to not be caught sleeping?
  C. What are some things that distract us from being alert?
  D. What can we do to stay awake, keep watch or be alert?
III. So what?
  A. How will your life be different because of the hope of the book of Revelation?
  B. In what areas do you need to be more alert?
  C. How will you change your life to be more ready and alert for His return?
IV. Conclusion: What would change for you?

Explain: **Jesus is coming back someday. We don't know when, but we do know He will return. Since Jesus is coming back soon, we have to live like He is going to be pulling into the driveway any moment and that means dedicating our lives to loving God by serving others.**

- Give each student a 3x5-inch card and a pen or pencil. Have them write their answer to the following question on the card:

If you knew that Jesus was going to come back in one year, what in your life would change?

Prayer and Commitment Time

- After students are finished writing their answers, lead them in a prayer of commitment to put their answers into action. Then have students demonstrate their commitment by putting their cards in their Bibles as bookmarks so that when they open God's Word, they will be reminded of their commitment.

REACT
SESSION THREE

Who Are Our Neighbors?

- Have students join their assigned REACT group. Instruct them to read Luke 10:29-37.
- Give each group a piece of poster board and felt-tip pens and instruct them to list as many of the people that they can think of in your area whom your youth group could serve in Jesus' name and how they could serve them.
- After they have made their lists, ask each group to choose one project and make plans to do it as a group within two weeks after returning from the retreat. They need to make their plans now to make sure they complete their service projects.
- Have them illustrate or explain the project they chose on the other side of their poster board.
- Tape the posters around the central meeting room and have a representative from each group tell the entire group about their project and their group's commitment to that project.

Worship Service: Being Heavenly Minded

Objective

Students will discover that even though much about the future is uncertain, there is something about the future that we can know for certain: Every believer's ultimate future is in heaven. That incredible fact can help us deal with living every day.

Biblical Basis

Acts 6:8—7:1; 7:55-60

Introduction: A Conference in Hell

Read the following illustration:

> It is said that a long time ago there was a conference in hell. And ol' Lucifer was plotting and scheming how he might catch the human race and keep them from God.
>
> One fiendish lieutenant came to the master of evil and said, "If you will send me to earth, I will tell the people that there is no heaven to be gained."
>
> Lucifer said to him, "No, no! They'll never believe it because there is a little bit of heaven in every heart."
>
> Another fiend came forward, darker and fouler than the first, and he said to Lucifer, "If you would send me to earth, I would convince the people that they can sin with immunity. That God would continue to love and forgive. That He would never, ever, ever judge anyone—even if they didn't repent. I will convince them of that."
>
> The father of darkness said, "No! These humans must not be underestimated. They have a conscience and deep within the heart of every earthling is this sense of righteousness. Beneath all their protestations they know that evil will be punished. They know that good will triumph over evil."
>
> A third lieutenant, from the very darkest pit emerged into the shadow of Lucifer's countenance and said,

"Master, if you would send me, I would tell them this:
'There is no hurry!' "
   And Lucifer said, "Go."[3]

Explain: **Most people think that the life they are living is all there is
and miss the fact that for those who are believers in Jesus, there is a
life to come that will make this one look sad in comparison. This
weekend we have talked a lot about the future: about your future,
about the future that the Bible predicts and about Jesus' return
someday. The truth is...**

1. I don't know anything about your future, and I don't believe
   in the psychic hotline and neither should you!
2. I don't understand everything about what the Bible says
   about the future.
3. I do know two things for sure about the future:
   a. Jesus is going to physically return to the earth someday,
      somewhere.
   b. If you are a believer in Jesus and you have asked Jesus to
      be your Savior, you are going to spend eternity in heaven
      with Him.

In the Word: Two Truths to Remind You About Heaven

I. The truth about heaven
   Read Acts 6:8—7:1; 7:55-60.
   A. Truth One: Being heavenly minded helps us to remember
      where our home is.
      1. In the story of Stephen, he looked up while he was being
         stoned. What did he see? (He saw Jesus and the glory of
         God.)
      2. The place you call "home" is important. Home is where
         you store your treasures—the things important to you. Is
         your permanent home here on earth or is it in heaven?
         Where *are* your treasures stored?
      3. The things we do during our lives reveal what we treasure. If
         you spend your time, money and energy on things that only
         matter here on earth, you've forgotten where your home is.
   B. Truth Two: Being heavenly minded helps us to deal with the
      rocks—the hard places in our lives.

Read Acts 7:58-60.

1. What kind of rocks are being thrown at you in your life?
    a. Do you have a tough family situation?
    b. Are you are struggling with an addiction?
    c. Do you have a physical, mental or emotional illness?
    d. Does a poor self-image prevent you from taking the risks to try anything, causing you to stop growing?
2. You're not alone. We all have rocks in our lives.
3. Knowing that heaven is in our futures can enable us to face the bad times and to enjoy the good things in our lives right now.

II. Conclusion
    A. I don't know what is going to happen in your future.
    B. I don't know when Jesus is coming back. He could come back before we go to bed or He could come back 1,000 years from now.
    C. I do know that I am going to see Jesus face-to-face someday soon. That's the hope I have as a believer in Jesus. Do you have the same hope?

Explain: **This weekend we talked a lot about the future. I hope you haven't gotten lost in everything else this weekend and forgotten about heaven. If you have never asked Jesus into your heart, this weekend would be a great time to do that. If you are a believer in Jesus, don't forget that Jesus is going to come back. Don't forget about the incredible gift that is yours to open someday—the gift of heaven.**

Our Response to God

- Attach the "Hangin' onto Heaven" poster to a wall in the room before the meeting begins.
- Give each person three gray sheets of construction paper cut to look like rocks. Ask each person to write on each rock one area in his or her life that pulls his or her focus away from heaven.
- Explain: **It has been great getting away together this weekend, but we all know that as soon as we get home, the rocks are going to start to hit us again. The challenge is to remember the fact that because there is a heaven and our God is in heaven, we can deal with the rocks in our lives. I want to take a minute and give you some time to talk with your heavenly Father about the rocks in your life and in your hand.**

- Pause for a minute or two to allow students to pray; then continue: **As a symbol of turning these rocks over to God and letting God deal with them, I am going to give you an opportunity to respond to God's word by taping your rocks on the "Hangin' onto Heaven" poster. I know this is just a symbol, but as you tape the rocks on the poster I hope it represents that you are putting your hurts in the hands of God.**

- Play quiet worship music or have group members sing an appropriate song as they tape their "rocks" to the poster board.
- Conclude with prayer.

Debriefing Session

- Have a time for students to reflect on the weekend and what they learned. This can be done just before you leave the retreat or when you return home. If you wait to debrief upon your return, do it before students leave for their homes.
- See page 12 in the Retreat Guidelines section for debriefing session ideas.

Notes
1. Adapted from Mike DeVries, *The Word on the New Testament* (Ventura, CA: Gospel Light, 1996) p. 161.
2. Ibid., pp. 162, 164-167.
3. Jim Burns and Greg McKinnon, *Illustrations, Stories and Quotes to Hang Your Message On* (Ventura, CA: Gospel Light, 1997) pp. 87-88.

What About You in 10, 20, 30 Years?

In 10 years

1. What work will you be doing? (If you will still be in school, where will you be going to school and what will your major be?)

2. What will your marital status be?

   Any kids?

3. What will you be driving?

4. What will your hobbies be?

In 20 years

1. What work will you be doing?

2. What will your marital status be?

   Any kids?

3. Where will you be living?

4. What will your home be like?

In 30 years

1. What work will you be doing?

2. What changes will have occurred in your life in the last 10 years?

3. What kind of church will you attend? What ministry will you be involved in?

4. What kind of place (rural, suburban, urban/apartment, condo, house) will you be living in? Name the place if you want!

5. What would you hope would be your greatest accomplishment over the past 30 years?

Experiencing Joy

The Big Idea

The purpose of this retreat is to help students learn how to experience the joy that we receive through the grace of God no matter what our circumstances. They will learn why and how joy comes to those who trust in Jesus.

Key Verses

"We also rejoice in our sufferings, because we know that suffering produces perseverance; perseverance, character; and character, hope. And hope does not disappoint us, because God has poured out his love into our hearts by the Holy Spirit, whom he has given us." Romans 5:3-5

Aims

During this retreat, you will guide students to:
*   Examine what true joy is through Jesus Christ;
*   Discover how we experience joy as a part of the new identity we have in salvation through Jesus Christ;
*   Implement action steps toward experiencing joy in the midst of any circumstance.

Location

Any camping or retreat facility within one to two hours from your church.

Time Frame

Friday evening to Sunday afternoon

Advance Preparation

❑ Organize student leadership teams at least one month before the retreat. Assign an adult leader to oversee each team. See the Retreat Guidelines section on page 11 for suggestions. Suggested teams for this retreat include:
- Transportation
- Bon Appetit
- Equipment
- Focus

❑ Set up small groups (five to six students per group) and assign each group an adult leader to facilitate discussions.

❑ Create two poster board signs, one that says "Agree" and one that says "Disagree."

❑ Obtain a video with highlights of the 1996 Olympics in Atlanta where Michael Johnson wins the 200-meter race.

❑ Arrange the use of a VCR and TV at the retreat facility. If one is not available, make arrangements to bring a portable TV and VCR.

❑ Prepare a slide or video show of growing children. Arrange the use of a slide projector if using slides.

❑ For Session Four: "Team Effort: Living in the Pressure Cooker," interview a few students on videotape. Ask them the following questions and record their responses on videotape:
1. What are some of the pressures you face as a teenager today?
2. How would you define the word "peace"?
3. Why does our world and people's lives seem to lack true peace?

❑ Photocopy reproducible student pages:
- "All for One and One for All" (p. 82)
- "Live the Thrill—Walk the Talk" (p. 83)
- "Running the Race" (p. 84)
- "Peace: It's Not Just for the 60s" (p. 85)

❑ Obtain signed medical and liability release forms from each retreat participant.

❑ Meet with leaders to finalize retreat schedule.

What Leaders Need to Bring

- ❏ Paper and pens/pencils
- ❏ "Agree" and "Disagree" poster boards
- ❏ Olympic highlights video
- ❏ Slides or video of growing children
- ❏ Portable TV and VCR, if none available at facility
- ❏ Slide projector and screen, if using slides
- ❏ Photocopies of student pages
- ❏ Signed copies of medical and liability release forms
- ❏
- ❏
- ❏

What Students Need to Bring

- ❏ Sleeping bag and pillow
- ❏ Appropriate clothing
- ❏ Toiletries
- ❏ Bible
- ❏ Notebook
- ❏ Pen or pencil
- ❏
- ❏
- ❏

Retreat Schedule

Friday

7:30 P.M.	Arrive at retreat site and get settled
8:30 P.M.	Worship
9:00 P.M.	Session One: All for One and One for All
9:30 P.M.	Small-group assignments and introductions
10:00 P.M.	Hang Time: crowdbreakers and games*
11:00 P.M.	In bed
11:30 P.M.	Lights out

Saturday

7:30 A.M.	Wake up
8:00 A.M.	Breakfast
8:30 A.M.	Quiet time and reflection
9:00 A.M.	Worship
9:30 A.M.	Session Two: Live the Thrill—Walk the Talk
10:30 A.M.	Small-group discussion
11:00 A.M.	Free time*
12:00 P.M.	Lunch
1:00 P.M.	Group activities/free time*
5:30 P.M.	Dinner
6:30 P.M.	Worship
7:00 P.M.	Session Three: Running the Race
8:00 P.M.	Small-group discussion
8:30 P.M.	Campfire program
9:30 P.M.	Hang Time: group games*
11:00 P.M.	In bed
11:30 P.M.	Lights out

Sunday

7:30 A.M.	Wake up
8:00 A.M.	Breakfast
8:30 A.M.	Quiet time and reflection
9:00 A.M.	Worship
9:30 A.M.	Session Four: Peace—It's Not Just for the 60s

10:30 A.M.	Small-group discussion
11:00 A.M.	Pack and load
12:00 P.M.	Lunch
1:00 P.M.	Depart for home

*Hang Time, Crowdbreaker, Game and Free Time Suggestions: Too much unstructured free time can lead to mischief or other problems. As a part of free times, be sure to plan some all-group activities, such as hiking, volleyball, softball or any other organized recreation. You can also add some creative activities and games: some that are simply fun activities, some that will build community, or some that will even teach a point. These activities and games are great for adding a sense of fun and adventure while building some great memories and group camaraderie. See the Retreat Guidelines section on page 14 for great resources to aid you in planning activities and games.

The Plan

Experiencing Joy

Session One:
All for One and
One for All

Objective

To introduce students to the partnership all believers share through our unity in Christ Jesus and to the variety of gifts we receive because of Christ's work on the Cross.

Biblical Basis

Romans 3:23; Philippians 1:1-11

Team Effort: Growing Up

- If you have children, or know someone who has small children, gather baby photos of the children. Have them made into slides or a video and show them at the beginning of the session.
- Talk about the radical changes that take place after a baby is born. Make the following points:
  1. When a baby is born, everything is new. There's no going back!
  2. The baby is in a new relationship with his or her mother and the environment.
  3. The baby now belongs to a new community—our society.
  4. The baby needs to be continually cared for, loved, held, fed, changed, etc.
- Talk about what it takes for a child to grow. Relate that to starting a new life with Jesus Christ.

- Explain: **The Bible says that we have all sinned and fall short of the glory of God (Romans 3:23). We are all born with sinful natures. At birth we all share in that original sin. But all is not lost. Through faith in Jesus Christ—being born again—we can leave our relationship with sin and become partners in Christ's gospel. By accepting Christ's work on the Cross, we are given complete forgiveness of our sins. We can become clean and share together in spreading the good news. In the opening verses in Philippians, Paul explained about the three gifts we receive when we are born again into God's family and become partners in the gospel.**

In the Word: God's Gifts to Us

Read Philippians 1:1-11.

I. Gift One: We receive a new status.
   A. We are "in Christ Jesus" (v. 1).
      1. We have accepted Him as our personal Savior and Lord and we have begun a relationship with Him.
      2. Through our relationship with Jesus, we receive His blessings of forgiveness and redemption.
   B. We are looked at by God as clean and holy.
   C. We are no longer seen as enemies and sinners, but we are seen by God as Jesus Christ is.

II. Gift Two: We receive a new life.
   A. "He [God] who began a good work in you will carry it on to completion until the day of Christ Jesus" (v. 6).
      1. When we are born again and start a relationship with Jesus, our hearts really have been changed from the inside.
      2. Our lives have been transformed, not just added to or put back together.
   B. The life that we live is no longer our own; it belongs to Christ.
      1. We have given control of our lives over to Jesus.
      2. He's no longer in the passenger's seat or outside the car. He's in the driver's seat.

III. Gift Three: We receive a new community.
   A. "All of you share in God's grace with me" (v. 7).
      1. We have moved from a community of sinners *without* salvation into a community that shares in the salvation of Jesus.

2. When we accept Christ as Savior, we automatically become one with other believers.

B. This new community supports us, encourages us and holds us accountable.

C. As a part of this new community, we're called to love one another, care for one another and walk this new life together.

Small-Group Discussion

- Have students join their assigned small groups.
- Give each student a copy of the Session One discussion questions (p. 82) and a pen or pencil.
- Instruct groups to discuss the questions.
- Close in prayer. Be sensitive to those students who need to begin a relationship with Christ or need to turn some area of their lives over to Him.

Session Two:
Live the Thrill—
Walk the Talk

Objective

To help students understand that by conducting themselves in a godly manner they, and others around them, can experience true joy.

Biblical Basis

Philippians 2:1-5,14,15

Team Effort: Why Didn't I Think of That?!?

- Divide the meeting room in half.
- On one side of the room put a piece of poster board that reads "Agree" and on the other side of the room a piece of poster board that reads "Disagree."
- Read the following statements and instruct students to move to the side of the room that best represents their opinion. Ask a few students to express their reasons for their choices.

1. I am joyful most of the time.
2. Joy should be something you have regardless of your situation.
3. As a Christian, you should be full of joy.
4. I should do whatever I want, regardless of those around me.
5. What I do affects those around me.
6. I can have an impact on the joy that others experience.

- After the experience, lead into the lesson by talking about how we conduct ourselves and the positive or negative impact our conduct can have on others.

- Explain: **Think for a moment about the past week at school. How did those with whom you came into contact treat you? Were you treated fairly in every case? Who treated you with love, kindness, goodness and encouragement? How did that make you feel? Did you feel joy because of how people treated you? Paul reminds us that the way we live our lives impacts those around us. When we live our lives according to God's Word, our joy becomes contagious.**

In the Word: The Truths and Our Responses

Read Philippians 2:1-5.

I. The Truth: "If" Statements

A. Philippians begins with several "if/then" statements—Paul's way of encouraging the Philippians with the truth of what they have. These "if" statements can also be translated "since."

B. There are four truths about what Christians have in being a part of Christ's Body (v. 1):

1. Truth One: Encouragement from being united with Christ
2. Truth Two: Comfort from His love
3. Truth Three: Fellowship with His Spirit
4. Truth Four: Tenderness and compassion

II. The Response: "Then" Statements

A. The following characteristics are six responses that will naturally result from our relationship with God.

B. Since we have these things, we should be living according to the following six "then" responses.

1. Response One: Be like-minded (v. 2).
2. Response Two: Have the same love as Christ (v. 2).
3. Response Three: Be one in spirit and purpose (v. 2).

4. Response Four: Do nothing out of selfish ambition or vain conceit (v. 3).
5. Response Five: In humility, consider others better than yourselves (v. 3).
6. Response Six: Look not only to your own interests but also to the interests of others (v. 4).

Small-Group Discussion

- Have students join their assigned small groups.
- Give each student a copy of the Session Two discussion questions (p. 83) and a pen or pencil.
- Instruct groups to discuss the questions.
- Close in prayer.

Session Three: Running the Race

Objective

To give students practical keys for living their lives as new creations.

Biblical Basis

Romans 8:38,39; Philippians 3:12-14; Hebrews 12:1,2

Team Effort: The Road to Glory

- Set up the video of the 1996 Olympic highlights. Cue the section of Michael Johnson winning the 200-meter race.
- Show the video clip; then discuss the following questions, writing the group's responses on a piece of poster board or on an overhead projector transparency.
  1. What makes Michael Johnson a great runner?
  2. What makes him an Olympic champion?
  3. What do you think are some of the costs he has had to pay to get where he is?
  4. What role have goals played in his winning the gold medal?
  5. How do you think winning a gold medal in the 200 is like running the race of the Christian life?

- Explain: **When we accept Christ as Savior, we need to understand that we are part of a new community in Christ and as part of that community God requires us to live up to high standards of conduct. How do we begin living as new creations? What does it take to run the race? Remember, our hearts have been changed by the forgiveness and redemption of Jesus. Where do we go from here? What now? Through his personal testimony, Paul has given us some hints for starting to live as "new creations" and run the race to win.**

In the Word: Jumping the Hurdles

Read Philippians 3:12-14. Explain: **These verses challenge us to press on toward the goal of living as God requires. There are four hurdles we need to clear in our quest toward the goal.**

I. Hurdle One: Recognize who and what we are.
   A. We are all sinners no matter whether we've accepted Christ or not.
   B. We aren't perfect, nor will we ever be this side of heaven.
   C. Remember that we have the power of the Holy Spirit to help us live our lives for Christ.
   D. We are not perfect, but our perfect God loves us and promises to give us the strength to make it.

II. Hurdle Two: Leave the past behind.
   A. We all have varied pasts.
      1. For many of us those pasts aren't something we want to share. We are embarrassed and ashamed of the things we were involved in or that we've done.
      2. Remember, after receiving Christ, we not only get a new life, but we can also leave the old one behind with His help.
      3. God's love is not based on what we do or have done in our lives; it is based on who we are.
   B. There is nothing in our past (or our present and our future) that will make God love you any less (see Romans 8:38,39).

III. Hurdle Three: Have a goal for the present.
   A. "If you aim at nothing, you're sure to hit it every time." If we want to achieve anything in our lives, we must know what it is that we are working toward achieving.
   B. Set your goal on Christ; let Him be your target (see Hebrews 12:1,2).

IV. Hurdle Four: Concentrate on the prize for the future.
   A. An intimate relationship with the holy, awesome Creator of the universe—the God that loves and cherishes you and me—that's our prize!
   B. Keep your eyes fixed on Jesus and you're sure to be motivated to continue running.
   C. As you focus on the finish line, all distractions will fade away.

Small-Group Discussion

*   Have students join their assigned small groups.
*   Give each student a copy of the Session Three discussion questions (p. 84) and a pen or pencil.
*   Instruct groups to discuss the questions.
*   Close in prayer, asking the students to pray for the strength to choose to live in the joy of the Lord.

Session Four: Peace—It's Not Just for the 60s

Objective

To encourage students to live a joyful life through the peace of God.

Biblical Basis

Philippians 4:4-13

Team Effort: Living in the Pressure Cooker

*   Show the interviews you prepared beforehand; then explain: **All it takes is a flip around the TV channels to find out that our world is in desperate need of peace. True peace is something our world is dying for—not a temporal peace but a peace of the soul, something eternal. There is a need for peace in our lives and that peace is available through Christ.**

In the Word: The Ingredients

Read Philippians 4:4-8.

I. The true ingredients for living in the joy and peace of the Lord include:

   A. Ingredient One: Trust in the Lord always (v. 4).

   B. Ingredient Two: Triumph over anxiousness (v. 6).

   C. Ingredient Three: Turn everything over to God in prayer (v. 6).

II. How do you do it?

   Explain: **Paul has the answer for us. He says that we need an attitude adjustment. Our attitudes and focus must be adjusted in order to receive God's gift of joy and peace. In Philippians 4, Paul gives us three targets to focus on!**

   Read Philippians 4:8-13.

   A. Target One: Focus your mind (v. 8).

   Focus your mind on whatever is true, noble, right, pure, lovely, admirable, excellent and praiseworthy.

   B. Target Two: Focus your eyes (v. 9).

   Focus your eyes on God's Word and the instruction it gives. Godly examples from Scripture and real life can help you survive the storms that come your way.

   C. Target Three: Focus your strength (v. 13).

   Focus on the strength God has for you. You may feel totally unable, but God's strength is able to help you tackle anything He calls you to do; it's His strength that will work in and through you.

Small-Group Discussion

- Have students join their assigned small groups.
- Give each student a copy of the Session Four discussion questions (p. 85) and a pen or pencil.
- Instruct groups to discuss the questions.
- Close in prayer.

Debriefing Session

- Have a time for students to reflect on the weekend and what they learned. This can be done just before you leave the retreat or when

you return home. If you wait to debrief upon your return, do it before students leave for their homes.

• See page 12 in the Retreat Guidelines section for debriefing session ideas.

Discussion Starters

Session One: All for One and One for All

Read Philippians 1:1-11.

1. What does it mean to "be in Christ Jesus"?

2. What are three gifts we receive by beginning a relationship with Christ?

3. What is required of you to receive those gifts?

4. How does it make you feel to know that you are part of this new community—the Body of Christ?

   Do you feel a part of the community? Why or why not?

5. Which of the three gifts do you struggle with the most or is hardest to realize the most in your life?

Discussion Starters

Session Two: Live the Thrill—Walk the Talk

Read Philippians 2:1-15.

1. Which of the six responses do you struggle with the most (see vv. 2,4)?

2. What are some of Jesus' characteristics according to verses 6 through 11?

3. What are some steps that you need to take to live what you say you believe?

4. On a scale of 1 to 10, 10 being incredibly joyful and 1 being incredibly joyless, where are you?

5. How would you define the word "joy"?

6. How would you respond to the following statement: "Times of greatest difficulty are also times of greatest joy"?

Close in prayer.

Discussion Starters

Session Three: Running the Race

Read Philippians 3:1-16.

1. Which of the four hurdles seems to trip you up as you run—recognizing who and what you are; leaving the past behind; having a goal for the present; or concentrating on the prize for the future?

2. How does our attitude in running the race affect our joy?

3. What does Romans 8:38,39 mean to you?

4. What does Hebrews 12:1,2 mean to you?

5. How would you respond to this statement: "Joy is a choice, not simply an emotional response"?

6. What are three action steps you need to take to make it over the four hurdles and live life joyfully?

Discussion Starters

Session Four: Peace—It's Not Just for the 60s

Read Philippians 4:4-8.

1. Why is it important to focus our minds and what we think about on the good things listed in verse 8?

2. What is Paul's secret for being content and experiencing joy in every situation?

3. What is one of the most difficult situations you've faced in the past year?

   How did God strengthen you through that time?

   What did you learn from the situation?

4. What have you learned this weekend that will help you experience joy in your life with Christ?

Prayer and Service: Putting It All Together

The Big Idea

Always pray and be willing to be the answer! Praying results in acting upon what God has put upon a person's heart. Learn the importance of both prayer and service by building a house for someone.

Key Verse

"Do not be anxious about anything, but in everything, by prayer and petition, with thanksgiving, present your requests to God." Philippians 4:6

Aims

During this retreat, you will guide students to:
• Examine what it means to pray and serve;
• Discover hindrances to prayer and the importance of being the answer to prayer;
• Implement their personal prayer life by building a house for a family that has been praying for it.

Location

Find a house-building missions facility in Mexico or the United States that can house your students. You will need to do some groundwork to find a location and project for this retreat. This can be done in Mexico through Amor Ministries at (714) 680-6401 or Mexico Caravan at (619) 569-8190. You could also contact Habitat for Humanity (1-800-334-3308) or another housing ministry or project in an area near you.

Time Frame

Friday evening through Sunday afternoon, plus any travel time needed

Budget

$30 to $50 per person for the weekend, plus travel expenses; $450 per house can be raised prior to the trip.

Advance Preparation

Please Note: If you are going out of the country, find out what form of identification (birth certificate, passport, school picture identification card or driver's license) is required. The missionaries or agency for which you are working would be the best source of information.

❑ Contact and arrange a visit with a home-building ministry.

❑ Organize student leadership teams at least one month before the retreat. Assign an adult leader to oversee each team. See the Retreat Guidelines section on page 11 for suggestions. Suggested teams for this retreat include:
  • Transportation
  • Bon Appetit—Arrange for parents to accompany the group with the primary ministry of supervising this team in meal preparations.
  • Equipment
  • Focus
  • Recreation

❑ Prepare and arrange training session two weeks before the retreat.

❑ Set up JAM Session groups (five to six students per group) and assign an adult leader to each group to facilitate discussions.

❑ Photocopy JAM Session handouts (pp. 102-106).

❑ Obtain foot-washing supplies:
  • Several plastic dishpans;
  • A gallon jug of water for every two participants (ask each student to bring an extra gallon of water);
  • Several bars of soap;
  • Washcloths and towels (have students provide their own);
  • Disposable facial tissues.

❑ Obtain signed medical and liability release forms from each retreat participant.

❑ Meet with leaders to finalize retreat schedule.

❑ For impromptu skits in Session One, prepare 3x5-inch cards with one of the following descriptions on a separate card:
  1. You ditch your friend in the mall.
  2. You allow your car to be more important than your friends.
  3. You gossip about your friend. (**Note:** It should not be real gossip.)
  4. You won't forgive your friend for something that he or she did wrong.
  5. You steal something from a friend that he or she really likes.

6. You do something to your friend out of wrong motives.

7. You act as though someone else is more important than your friend.

8. When your friend asks for forgiveness, you don't forgive and just remind him or her how much it hurt you and that you could never forgive him/her for doing such a thing.

❑ Bring housewarming gifts for the new home.

❑

❑

❑

What Leaders Need to Bring

- ❑ JAM Session photocopies
- ❑ Paper and pens/pencils
- ❑ 3x5-inch cards
- ❑ White board and markers; chalkboard and chalk; or overhead screen, transparencies and markers
- ❑ Footwashing supplies
- ❑ 3x5-inch prepared cards for Session One
- ❑ Gifts for the new home
- ❑ Signed copies of medical and liability release forms, one from each student
- ❑ Personal identification (driver's license, school ID, passport, etc.)
- ❑
- ❑
- ❑

What Students Need to Bring

- ❑ Sleeping bag and pillow
- ❑ Toiletries
- ❑ Appetite and smiles
- ❑ Extra money for the round trip
- ❑ Bible
- ❑ Prayer journal
- ❑ Student leadership notebook
- ❑ Pens/pencils
- ❑ Bottled water with your name on it (Reminder: Do NOT share!)
- ❑ Baby wipes
- ❑ Work gloves and sturdy shoes
- ❑ Rain gear
- ❑ Hammers/nail bags/screwdrivers
- ❑ Medical and liability release forms
- ❑ Duffle bag
- ❑ Backpack
- ❑ Personal identification (driver's license, school ID, passport, etc.)
- ❑
- ❑
- ❑

Training Guidelines

Discuss the following with students and adult leaders two weeks prior to the event:

1. Have students write out their testimonies.
2. Explain what the missions trip is all about.
3. Have the missions committee or pastor speak to the group.
4. Go over common Spanish phrases (if appropriate).
5. Introduce the interpreters.
6. Review Student Leadership Teams and their duties:
   a. Transportation
   b. Equipment
   c. Bon Appetit
   d. Focus
7. Review the following requirements and standards:
   a. Clothing requirements—what to wear and what *not* to wear
   b. Water/food—what to drink/eat and what *not* to drink/eat
   c. Luggage
   d. Health and safety precautions
   e. Bathroom facilities
   f. Who is in charge
   g. What to do if you get separated from the group
   h. Border crossing—if going to Mexico or outside of the country
   i. Buddy system—three or more students with an adult
   j. Tools
   k. Standards for boy/girl conduct
   l. General conduct/youth group rules
   m. Respecting culture/community
   n. Departure and return times
8. Organize prayer teams:
   a. Divide students and adult leaders into prayer teams;
   b. Instruct teams to pray for each member weekly before the event and daily during the event.
9. Have a question and answer time.
10. Hand out medical/liability release forms and emergency information sheets that students need to keep with them at all times.
11. Discuss what to bring (see list on preceding page).
12. Discuss what *not* to bring.

Retreat Schedule

Sunday—two weeks prior to trip

3:00-6:00 P.M.   Training meeting

Friday

*2:00 P.M.   Registration and departure (student leadership teams assist)

*3:00 P.M.   Leave

*7:00 P.M.   Arrive at the border

Dinner at a fast-food restaurant, stateside

Meet missionary at Mexican Insurance Agency

*8:00 P.M.   Cross border with missionary

*9:00 P.M.   Arrive at the missions site

*9:20 P.M.   JAM Session One

10:00 P.M.   Lights out

Saturday

6:30 A.M.   Personal devotions

7:00 A.M.   Breakfast (Bon Appetit Team)

Pack sack lunches for project site

8:00 A.M.   Session One: Prayer

8:45 P.M.   JAM Session Two

9:30 A.M.   Leave for home building project

10:00 A.M.   Arrive at home building project

12:30 P.M.   Lunch on site with the family

1:00 P.M.   JAM Session Three

1:30 P.M.   Finish home building project

5:00 P.M.   Head back to mission housing facility

5:30 P.M.   Arrive at housing facility, free time until dinner

6:30 P.M.   Dinner (Bon Appetit Team)

7:15 P.M.   Session Two: The Importance of Serving

8:00 P.M.   JAM Session Four

9:00 P.M.   Snack time

10:00 P.M.   Lights out

Sunday

6:30 A.M.	Personal devotions
7:00 A.M.	Breakfast (Bon Appetit Team)
8:00 A.M.	JAM Session Five
9:00 A.M.	Worship and prayer time
10:00 A.M.	Pack up for the border and clean the facility
*11:00 A.M.	Depart
*1:00 P.M.	Cross the border and have lunch.

*Times approximate depending on the length of your trip.

The Plan

Prayer and Service: Putting It All Together

JAM SESSION ONE

Before lights out:
- Gather everyone around the campfire or in the meeting area.
- If you have not done so before leaving for the retreat, assign students to their JAM Session groups. They will return to their assigned groups throughout the retreat.
- Have students join their assigned JAM Session groups.
- Hand out JAM Session One questions. Have the groups discuss the questions.
- Have each group share their answers with the whole group.
- Have the worship leaders sing a few songs and close the night in a discipline of silence, encouraging students to go to bed talking to God.

Session One: Prayer

Objective

During this session, you will guide students to:
- Examine the five things that hinder prayer;
- Discover how to eliminate those five things;
- Implement ways to be more effective in their prayer life.

Biblical Basis

Deuteronomy 6:14,15; Psalm 66:18-20; 119:11; Proverbs 21:13; Ezekiel 14:7,8; Amos 5:14; Matthew 5:8; Mark 11:25; 2 Corinthians 9:7; Ephesians 4:32; Philippians 4:6; James 4:3; 1 John 1:8—2:1

Key Verse

"Do not be anxious about anything, but in everything, by prayer and petition, with thanksgiving, present your requests to God." Philippians 4:6

Warm-Up: How to Mess Up a Good Relationship

- Ask several volunteers to do impromptu skits. Ask them to pair up and give each pair a 3x5-inch card with a description of one of the following situations.
    1. You ditch your friend in the mall.
    2. You allow your car to be more important than your friends.
    3. You gossip about your friend. (**Note:** It should not be real gossip.)
    4. You won't forgive your friend for something that he or she did wrong.
    5. You steal something from a friend that he or she really likes.
    6. You do something to your friend out of wrong motives.
    7. You act as though someone else is more important than your friend.
    8. When your friend asks for forgiveness, you don't forgive and just remind him or her how much it hurt you and that you could never forgive him/her for doing such a thing.
- Give them a few minutes to develop their skits.
- After each pair has done their brief skit before the group, say something like: **We often mess up our relationships with others, sometimes without knowing it. Let's brainstorm other ways that we mess up our relationships with other people.**

Team Effort: Messing Up

- Ask the group: **What are some ways that we can mess up a good relationship?**

- As students respond, have someone write their responses on a white board, chalkboard or overhead transparency.
- Explain: **You have shared some important things. Today we want to look at some ways that our relationship with God can be hurt, causing our prayers to be hindered.**

 BIG IDEA As Christians we are called to pray without ceasing, yet in the midst of prayer we need to realize that there are some things that can hinder our prayers.

In the Word: Five Roadblocks to Prayer

Read each of the following Scripture passages and share how each roadblock might hinder our prayers to God. Read the solution and share what we are to do to remove each roadblock.

I. Unconfessed Sin
  A. Roadblock
  "If I had cherished sin in my heart, the Lord would not have listened; but God has surely listened and heard my voice in prayer" (Psalm 66:18,19).
  B. Solutions
    1. "If we claim to be without sin, we deceive ourselves and the truth is not in us. If we confess our sins, he is faithful and just and will forgive us our sins and purify us from all unrighteousness" (1 John 1:8,9).
    2. "Seek good, not evil, that you may live. Then the Lord God Almighty will be with you, just as you say he is" (Amos 5:14).

II. Worship of Idols
  A. Roadblock
  "When any Israelite or any alien living in Israel separates himself from me and sets up idols in his heart and puts a wicked stumbling block before his face and then goes to a prophet to inquire of me, I the Lord will answer him myself. I will set my face against that man and make him an example and a byword. I will cut him off from my people. Then you will know that I am the Lord" (Ezekiel 14:7,8).
  B. Solution
  "Do not follow other gods, the gods of the peoples around you; for the Lord your God, who is among you, is a jealous

God and his anger will burn against you, and he will destroy you from the face of the land" (Deuteronomy 6:14,15).

III. Wrong Motives

    A. Roadblock

       "When you ask, you do not receive, because you ask with wrong motives, that you may spend what you get on your pleasures" (James 4:3).

    B. Solution

       1. "Blessed are the pure in heart, for they will see God" (Matthew 5:8).

       2. "I have hidden your word in my heart that I might not sin against you" (Psalm 119:11).

IV. Self-Centeredness/Greed

    A. Roadblock

       "If a man shuts his ears to the cry of the poor, he too will cry out and not be answered" (Proverbs 21:13).

    B. Solution

       "Each man should give what he has decided in his heart to give, not reluctantly or under compulsion, for God loves a cheerful giver" (2 Corinthians 9:7).

V. Unforgiveness

    A. Roadblock

       "When you stand praying, if you hold anything against anyone, forgive him, so that your Father in heaven may forgive you your sins" (Mark 11:25).

    B. Solution

       "Be kind and compassionate to one another, forgiving each other, just as in Christ God forgave you" (Ephesians 4:32).

Things to Think About

- Explain: **We have such a gracious and loving God. He has set up a simple plan for getting back into a right relationship with Him.** Read 1 John 1:8—2:1.
- Ask: **This was written to believers. What do we need to do when we sin?**
- Allow students some time to silently confess anything that might be a roadblock, hindering their prayer life.
- Close in corporate prayer.

JAM SESSION TWO

After Session One
- Have students join their assigned JAM Session groups.
- Hand out JAM Session Two questions. Have the groups discuss the questions.
- When the time is over, have them prepare for the home-building project.

JAM SESSION THREE

After Lunch
- Have students join their assigned JAM Session groups.
- Hand out JAM Session Three questions. Have the groups discuss the questions.

Session Two: Service Means Being Willing to Be the Answer!

Objective

During this session, you will guide students to:
- Examine what it means to be a servant;
- Discover ways to be a servant of God;
- Implement the evaluation of their attitudes about building a house for people or for God.

Biblical Basis

Joshua 24:24; Matthew 5:16; Mark 10:45; Luke 4:8; John 13:1-17; Galatians 5:13; 6:9; Ephesians 6:7,8; 1 Peter 2:12; 4:10

Key Verse

"Serve wholeheartedly, as if you were serving the Lord, not men, because you know that the Lord will reward everyone for whatever good he does, whether he is slave or free." Ephesians 6:7,8

Warm-Up: How Did It Go?

- Explain: **Today you spent time serving. What did you do and who did you do it for?**
- Have students give examples of how they served today. Remember to encourage the answers and praise them for what they did. Set them up to understand the message by being more encouraging to their responses about serving *people* rather than serving *God*.

We need to understand that we are not serving man, ideas or a ministry but the almighty, all-knowing and all-present God!

BIG IDEA

In the Word: Servant of God, Not Man!

- Explain: **Being a servant is not an easy thing to do, but we all need to serve in such a way that nonbelievers see a difference. Examine the following verses and ask yourself the question** *How does this apply to me?*
- Have students read Matthew 5:16 and 1 Peter 2:12.
- Explain: **These verses tell who we are called to serve. Read the following Scripture passages and write down who we are asked to serve.**
- Have selected students read Joshua 24:24; Luke 4:8; Galatians 5:13; 1 Peter 4:10.
- Explain: **When we serve people at church, school, work and other places sometimes it is really hard. It's a lot easier to serve when you understand that you're being called to serve.**
- Discuss the following:
  According to Mark 10:45, who is our example?
  When discouraged, we usually need to regain our perspective on serving. What do Galatians 6:9 and Ephesians 6:7 say about keeping our perspective in serving?
  What do you need to do in order to keep that idea in mind?

Things to Think About: Foot Washing—Being a Servant to All

Materials:
- Plastic dishpans and several gallon jugs of water
- Washcloths
- Soap
- Towels (Students could bring their own.)
- Bible
- Tissues

Preparation
- Have a method of discarding and replacing the water after each washing (to avoid spreading diseases).
- Have the equipment distributed around the room.
- Read John 13:1-17.
- Don't say anything after the passage is read. Just begin washing the feet of the other leaders.
- Challenge the group with the thought of verse 15, **"I have set you an example that you should do as I have done for you."**
- After all the leaders are done, have them wash the feet of the student leaders. Encourage students to then wash one another's feet as a model of what it means to be a servant.
- Close the session in a time of prayer and worship.

JAM SESSION FOUR

After Foot Washing
- Have students join their assigned JAM Session groups.
- Hand out JAM Session Four questions. Have the groups discuss the questions.

JAM SESSION FIVE

After Sunday Breakfast
- Have students join their assigned JAM Session groups.
- Hand out JAM Session Five questions. Have the groups discuss the questions.

- Before closing the JAM Session, share how proud you are of the accomplishments of each student.
- Close the small group session by having one representative from each small group pray.

Debriefing Session

- Have a time for students to reflect on the weekend and what they learned. This can be done just before you leave the retreat or when you return home. If you wait to debrief upon your return, do it before students leave for their homes.
- See page 12 in the Retreat Guidelines section for debriefing session ideas.

JAM Session One

Discuss the following questions and write down your answers:

1. Write the key verse for the weekend—Philippians 4:6.

2. List three specific things that you have been praying for about this weekend.

3. List three ways that you can help serve each other this weekend.

Spend several minutes in prayer asking God to help you and your group learn what it means to serve Him with your whole heart.

JAM Session Two

Discuss the following questions and write down your answers:

1. If you are going to rate your prayer life on a scale of 1 to 10 with 10 being awesome, what score would you give yourself?

2. Are there any reasons why God would not hear your prayers? What are they?

3. Why is prayer so important?

4. How can you encourage others to pray?

Take five minutes to write a prayer to God in your prayer journal.

JAM Session Three

Please consider the following questions and write down your answers:

1. How long do you think this family has been praying for a home?

   Circle one: 1 year   2 years   5 years   10+ years   never

2. List four reasons why it is important to serve others who are in need.

3. What are some needs that your friends back home have that we need to pray about?

   How can we serve them just as we are doing here?

4. List five people back home that have needs that we can be praying about and possibly take care of when we return home.

JAM Session Four

Discuss the following questions and write down your answers:

1. What did Jesus mean about being a servant (see Mark 10:45; John 13:14-16)?

   Give your definition of a servant.

2. List at least three ways that being a servant makes you a better leader.

3. Knowing Jesus and His life, list at least five ways that He served others.

4. Since serving others usually begins in the home, how can you better serve your family when you return from this trip? List at least five ways.

Spend 10 minutes in prayer asking God to make you a better servant. Use your prayer journal to write out your prayer and any thoughts that occur during your prayer time.

JAM Session Five

Discuss the following questions and write down your answers:

1. If you were going to ask God to do something back home, what would it be?

2. If you were going to do something back home for someone else, what would you do?

3. What are six things that you will remember from this weekend?

Pray for the families and friends that you've met this weekend.

Love, Sex, and Dating: How to Handle the Heat!

 This retreat is based on Jim Burns's material from *The Word on Sex, Drugs & Rock 'n' Roll*. It is designed to show how curriculum can be used in a retreat format. You will need to obtain a copy of the book for this retreat.

The Big Idea

Young people need to understand God's radical and wise plan for love, sex, dating and marriage and how to follow that plan in their relationships with the opposite sex.

Key Verses

"Flee from sexual immorality. All other sins a man commits are outside his body, but he who sins sexually sins against his own body. Do you not know that your body is a temple of the Holy Spirit, who is in you, whom you have received from God? You are not your own; you were bought at a price. Therefore honor God with your body." 1 Corinthians 6:18-20

Aims

During this retreat, you will guide students to:
- Examine God's standards for sexuality found in His Word;
- Discover God's principles for setting sexual standards in the context of real-life relationships;
- Implement a decision to take "The Sexual Purity Challenge" and honor God with their bodies.

Location

This retreat can take place at any camping area or retreat facility within an hour to an hour and a half of your church.

Time Frame

Friday evening through Sunday afternoon

Advance Preparation

Note: It is good to have a preretreat meeting with the parents of the students attending this retreat. At this meeting explain the weekend, review the lessons and related materials, and discuss how parents can follow up with their teens when they return from the retreat. You could also hand out the appropriate Parent Pages from *The Word on Sex, Drugs & Rock 'n' Roll* (pp. 29, 41, 57, 73) for parents to continue the discussions of the concepts at home. This will ease any concerns that parents may have about this sensitive subject, plus it will involve them in an active way in this important area of their teen's life.

❏ Obtain a copy of *The Word on Sex, Drugs & Rock 'n' Roll* by Jim Burns (Ventura, CA: Gospel Light, 1994).
❏ Photocopy the student pages from the study that you will be using:
  • Team Effort: The Word on Sex (p. 23)
  • In the Word: God's True View (p. 25)
  • Things to Think About (p. 27)
  • Team Effort: Who's Really Influencing Teens About Sex? (p. 35)
  • In the Word: God's Standards vs. the Movies (p. 37)
  • Things to Think About (p. 39)
  • Team Effort: How Far Should I Go? (p. 67)
  • In the Word: Showing True Love (p. 69)
  • Things to Think About (p. 71)
  • Choose one of the Team Efforts, (either p. 47 or p. 49)
  • In the Word: The Sexual Purity Challenge (pp. 51, 53)
  • Make cards of The Sexual Purity Pledge (p. 53), two for each student attending
  • Things to Think About (p. 55)
❏ Obtain any other materials needed for the lessons you select.
❏ Obtain signed medical and liability release forms from each retreat participant.
❏ Meet with leaders to finalize retreat schedule.
❏
❏
❏

What Leaders Need to Bring

- ❏ Paper and pens/pencils
- ❏ Photocopies of selected student pages
- ❏ *The Word on Sex, Drugs and Rock 'n' Roll*
- ❏ Signed copies of medical and liability release forms
- ❏
- ❏
- ❏

What Students Need to Bring

- ❏ Appropriate clothing
- ❏ Sleeping bag and pillow
- ❏ Toiletries
- ❏ Appetite and smiles
- ❏ Extra money
- ❏ Bible
- ❏ Prayer journal
- ❏ Student leadership notebook
- ❏ Pen or pencils
- ❏
- ❏
- ❏

Retreat Schedule

Friday

7:00 P.M.	Arrive and unpack
8:00 P.M.	Session One: Is God the Great Killjoy?
9:30 P.M.	Free time, snacks and social or recreation time*
10:30 P.M.	In rooms
11:00 P.M.	Lights out

Saturday

7:00 A.M.	Wake up
8:00 A.M.	Solo Time One
8:30 A.M.	Breakfast
9:00 A.M.	Session Two: Influences
10:30 A.M.	Free time*
12:00 P.M.	Lunch
1:00 P.M.	Free time group activity*
6:00 P.M.	Dinner
7:00 P.M.	Session Three: How Far Is Too Far?
9:00 P.M.	Free time, snacks and social or recreation time*
10:30 P.M.	In rooms
11:00 P.M.	Lights out

Sunday

7:00 A.M.	Wake up
8:00 A.M.	Solo Time Two
8:30 A.M.	Breakfast
9:00 A.M.	Clean up camp
9:30 A.M.	Session Four: Taking the Sexual Purity Challenge
11:00 A.M.	Pack vehicles, then free time*
12:00 P.M.	Lunch
1:00 P.M.	Leave for home

*Free Time Suggestions: Too much unstructured free time can lead to mischief or other problems. As a part of free times, be sure to plan

some all-group activities, such as hiking, volleyball, softball or any other organized recreation. You can also add creative activities and games: some simply fun activities, some that will build community, or some that will even teach a point. These activities and games are great for adding a sense of fun and adventure while building some great memories and group camaraderie. See the Retreat Guidelines section on page 14 for great resources to aid you in planning activities and games.

The Plan

Love, Sex, and Dating: How to Handle the Heat!

Session One: Is God the Great Killjoy?

Objectives

During this session, you will guide students to:
- Examine what the Bible says about sexuality;
- Discover that God cares deeply for them and has given them the gift of their sexuality;
- Thank God for His gift of sex and pray for a biblical understanding of sexuality.

Biblical Basis

Genesis 1:26,31; 2:18-25; Exodus 20:14; Matthew 19:4-6; Galatians 5:19,20; Philippians 2:3,4; Hebrews 13:4

Key Verse

"Then God said, 'Let us make man in our image, in our likeness, and let them rule over the fish of the sea and the birds of the air, over the livestock, over all the earth, and over all the creatures that move along the ground.' God saw all that he had made, and it was very good." Genesis 1:26,31

Praise and Worship

Start the session with a time of praise and worship.

Retreat Expectations

Start off the first session with a brief refresher of the retreat expectations. Be sure to minimize and express verbally and in writing what your expectations are. A good outline to use is the following:

The Four *M*s

1. Meals—You must be at all meals.
2. Meetings—You must be at all meetings.
3. Messing Around—You shouldn't be messing around: being in the rooms of the opposite sex, being where you don't belong, not being where you should be, etc.
4. Making Out—No intense physical relationships on the retreat, especially since we're talking about love, sex and dating.

> **BIG IDEA**
>
> God created sex and wants the best for us.

The Lesson: Is God the Great Killjoy?

- Use Session One: "Is God the Great Killjoy?" from *The Word on Sex, Drugs & Rock 'n' Roll* by Jim Burns on pages 17-29.
- Begin the teaching time with "Team Effort: The Word on Sex" (p. 23) for high school and continue on with "In the Word: God's True View" (p. 25). Use "So What?" and "Things to Think About" sections as small-group discussion starters.
- Close your session with another time of praise and worship.

SOLO TIME ONE

- Give each student a copy of the "Solo Time One" handout (p. 120) and a pen or pencil.
- Have each student spend 30 minutes alone with God, the handout, a Bible and a notebook.

Session Two: Influences

Objective

During this session, you will guide students to:

- Examine the media's influence on sexuality;
- Discover how the Bible's true view of sexuality differs from the media's view;
- Identify one way the media has negatively influenced them and make appropriate changes.

Biblical Basis

Matthew 5:27-30; Ephesians 5:3-5; 1 Thessalonians 4:1-8

Key Verse

"It is God's will that you should be sanctified: that you should avoid sexual immorality." 1 Thessalonians 4:3

Praise and Worship

Start the session with a time of praise and worship.

The Bible's view of sexuality and the media's view of sexuality differ. We need to discern between the two views. **BIG IDEA**

The Lesson: Influences

- Use Session Two: "Influences" from *The Word on Sex, Drugs and Rock 'n' Roll* by Jim Burns on pages 31-41.
- Begin with "Warm-Up: It's in Our Music Contest."
- Select a Team Effort, then continue on to "In the Word: God's Standards vs. the Movies."
- Use "So What?" and "Things to Think About" sections as small group discussion starters.
- Close the time in praise and worship.

Session Three: How Far Is Too Far?

Objective

During this session, you will guide students to:

- Examine the often-asked question: "How far is too far?";
- Discover God's principles for setting sexual standards;
- Set biblical sexual standards.

Biblical Basis

1 Corinthians 10:13; 13:4-7

Key Verse

"No temptation has seized you except what is common to man. And God is faithful; he will not let you be tempted beyond what you can bear. But when you are tempted, he will also provide a way out so that you can stand up under it." 1 Corinthians 10:13

Praise and Worship

Start the session with a time of praise and worship.

 BIG IDEA Young people need to set standards before they are in a tempting situation. The decisions they make today will affect them for a lifetime.

The Lesson: How Far Is Too Far?

- Use "How Far Is Too Far?" from *The Word on Sex, Drugs and Rock 'n' Roll* by Jim Burns (pp. 59-73).
- Begin the teaching time with "Team Effort: How Far Should I Go?" (p. 67), and continue with "In the Word: Showing True Love" (p. 69).
- Use "So What?" and "Things to Think About" sections for small group discussion starters.

- Close this time together in praise and worship.

> Be sensitive to students who may need to pray with someone about the issues raised in this session. There may be students who need to confess sin in their lives, seek forgiveness or just be reassured of God's love.

Solo Time Two

- Give each student a copy of the "Solo Time Two" handout (p. 121) and a pen or pencil.
- Have each student spend 30 minutes alone with God, the handout, a Bible and a notebook.

Session Four:
Taking the Sexual Purity Challenge

Objective

During this session, you will guide students to:
- Examine the possibility of living a life of sexual abstinence until marriage;
- Discover the biblical basis for giving their bodies and sexual standards to God;
- Implement a decision to take "The Sexual Purity Challenge" and honor God with their bodies.

Biblical Basis

1 Corinthians 6:18-20; Ephesians 5:1,3; 1 Thessalonians 4:1-8; 1 Peter 2:11

Key Verse

"Flee from sexual immorality. All other sins a man commits are outside

his body, but he who sins sexually sins against his own body. Do you not know that your body is a temple of the Holy Spirit, who is in you, whom you have received from God? You are not your own; you were bought at a price. Therefore honor God with your body." 1 Corinthians 6:18-20

Praise and Worship

Start the session with a time of praise and worship.

BIG IDEA Teens need to commit their bodies to God and refrain from sexual intercourse until marriage.

The Lesson: Taking the Sexual Purity Challenge

- Use "Taking the Sexual Purity Challenge" from *The Word on Sex, Drugs & Rock 'n' Roll* (pp. 43-57).
- Begin the teaching time with one of the Team Efforts (p. 47 or p. 49). Continue with "In the Word: The Sexual Purity Challenge" (pp. 51, 53).
- Have the small groups discuss "Things to Think About" (p. 55).
- Have "The Sexual Purity Pledge" (p. 53) prepared on small cards. Have students sign them.
- **For a variation:** Give each student two cards and two lines to sign on each card. Have students pair up with someone that they want to keep them accountable for their decision. Have the other person sign the card. The person holding the other individual accountable will keep the second signed card as a reminder to pray for that person.
- Close this time together in praise and worship.

Once again, be sensitive to the students in your group. You will want to reassure students who have already been sexually active that this challenge begins today, regardless of their past. Some students, again, may need to pray with an adult leader over issues brought up through the course of the weekend.

- Have students gather in their small groups and have them pray together to close this lesson and the retreat. Have them pray for each other and the commitments they have made to abstain from sex from this day until their wedding day.

Debriefing Session

- Have a time for students to reflect on the weekend and what they learned. This can be done just before you leave the retreat or when you return home. If you wait to debrief upon your return, do it before students leave for their homes.
- See page 12 in the Retreat Guidelines section for debriefing session ideas.

Solo Time One

Read Genesis 2:18-24.

1. Why did God create marriage?

2. What are the three basic aspects of marriage listed in verse 24?

3. Other than physical intimacy, what are other ways two people can become one?

4. Ask God to provide a man/woman for you who will share this same biblical understanding of marriage and to give you the patience to wait for this special someone.

Solo Time Two

Read Psalm 150.

1. What kinds of things do you and your friends talk about?

2. In what ways does this psalm tell us to praise God?

3. How do you offer praise to God?

4. What should motivate God's people to praise the Lord?

5. How has the Lord demonstrated His love for you?

Faith That Works

The Big Idea

There is a relationship between faith and works. There needs to be an understanding of how faith should make a difference in believers' lives and how faith needs to be lived out each day.

Key Verse

"You see that a person is justified by what he does and not by faith alone." James 2:24

Aims

During this retreat, you will guide students to:
- Examine what faith is all about and how to live by it;
- Discover the difference between works and faith and choose to live a life of faith;
- Implement an action plan for living a "faith-full" Christian life.

Location

This retreat can take place at any camping area or retreat facility within an hour to an hour and a half of your church.

Time Frame

Friday evening through Sunday afternoon

Advance Preparation

❑ Photocopy the small group discussion starters (pp. 141-144).

❑ Collect enough blindfolds for half the number of students who will be attending.

❑ Obtain materials needed for the Session Four obstacle course (see p. 138).

❑ Obtain a video of *Indiana Jones and the Last Crusade*, plus TV and VCR (if the retreat facility does not have these available).

❑ Prepare three sheets of poster board with one of the following written on each sheet: "Agree," "Disagree" and "I don't have a clue!"

❑ Set up small groups (five to six students per group) and assign each group an adult leader to facilitate discussions.

❑ Call retreat facility to arrange the use of a TV and VCR.

❑ Obtain signed medical and liability release forms from each retreat participant.

❑ Meet with leaders to finalize retreat schedule.

❑

❑

❑

What Leaders Need to Bring

- ❑ Paper and pens/pencils
- ❑ Blindfolds
- ❑ Obstacle course materials
- ❑ *Indiana Jones and the Last Crusade* video (and TV/VCR if needed)
- ❑ Prepared poster boards
- ❑ Signed copies of medical and liability release forms
- ❑
- ❑
- ❑

What Students Need to Bring

- ❑ Sleeping bag and pillow
- ❑ Appropriate clothing
- ❑ Toiletries
- ❑ Bible
- ❑ Notebook
- ❑ Pen or pencil
- ❑
- ❑
- ❑
- ❑

Retreat Schedule

Friday

7:30 P.M.	Arrive at retreat site and get settled
8:30 P.M.	Worship
9:00 P.M.	Session One: Faith That Works
9:30 P.M.	Small-group discussion
10:00 P.M.	Hang Time: games*
11:00 P.M.	In cabins
11:30 P.M.	Lights out

Saturday

7:30 A.M.	Wake up
8:00 A.M.	Breakfast
9:00 A.M.	Worship
9:30 A.M.	Session Two: Faith at Work in Trials and Temptations
10:30 A.M.	Small-group discussion
11:00 A.M.	Free time*
12:00 P.M.	Lunch
1:00 P.M.	Group activities/free time*
5:30 P.M.	Dinner
6:30 P.M.	Worship
7:00 P.M.	Session Three: Faith at Work in Actions
8:00 P.M.	Small-group discussion
8:30 P.M.	Campfire program
9:30 P.M.	Hang Time: group games and other activities*
11:00 P.M.	In bed
11:30 P.M.	Lights out

Sunday

7:30 A.M.	Wake up
8:00 A.M.	Breakfast
9:00 A.M.	Worship
9:30 A.M.	Session Four: Faith at Work in Relationships
10:30 A.M.	Small-group discussion
11:00 A.M.	Pack and load

12:00 P.M.   Lunch
1:00 P.M.   Depart for home

*Hang Time, Game and Free Time Suggestions: Too much unstructured free time can lead to mischief or other problems. As a part of free times, be sure to plan some all-group activities, such as hiking, volleyball, softball or any other organized recreation. You can also add some creative activities and games: some that are simply fun activities, some that will build community, or some that will even teach a point. These activities and games are great for adding a sense of fun and adventure while building some great memories and group camaraderie. See the Retreat Guidelines section on page 14 for great resources to aid you in planning activities and games.

The Plan

Faith That Works

Session One:
Faith That Works

Objective

To give students a definition of faith and what believers are assured through faith in Christ.

Biblical Basis

Matthew 1:18-25; 20:29-34; Luke 1:26-38,45; Romans 4:21; 2 Corinthians 5:7; Hebrews 11:1; James 2:17

Key Verse

"Now faith is being sure of what we hope for and certain of what we do not see." Hebrews 11:1

Team Effort: Walk by Faith

- Have everyone find a partner that they don't know well. Give them five minutes to find out as many things as they can that they have in common.
- Have the following pairs share with the whole group:
    1. The pair with the most things in common.
    2. The pair with the least things in common.
    3. The pair with the strangest thing in common.
- Have the pairs stay together. Give a blindfold to each pair.
- Have one person put the blindfold on the other person. The person

without the blindfold is to lead the person with the blindfold on a trust/faith walk. Have them walk around outside (set boundaries so you don't lose anyone!) for about five minutes. Then at a given signal (ring a bell or blow a whistle) have them change roles.

- Discuss the following questions when they return to the room:
  1. **What was the hardest thing about being blindfolded?**
  2. **Did you really trust the person? Why or why not?**
  3. **Was it tough to walk "by faith, not by sight"? What made it difficult?**
  4. **How does Hebrews 11:1 relate to our exercise?**
  5. **What are some of the ways that we need to walk "by faith, not by sight" in our relationship with God?**

In the Word: Faith in Action

Introduction

- Explain: **Faith requires action. It means stepping out, even when you don't know what's ahead of you.**
- Have the *Indiana Jones and the Last Crusade* video cued to begin where Indiana Jones makes his step of faith to get to the chamber with the Holy Grail, and stop the clip when he successfully crosses the cavern to get to the chamber.
- Introduce the video segment by explaining: **Faith is more than just a belief in something or someone, it's stepping out in action. What you are about to see is an example of what faith is. Faith is not just believing something, it's acting on what you believe.**
- Show the video clip, stopping the clip at the appropriate spot.
- After the video segment, indicate an imaginary line down the center of your room. Designate one side of your room the "agree" side and the other as the "disagree" side. Read the following statements and have students move to the side of the line that represents their opinions. Have some members of each opinion group discuss their opinions.
  1. **Seeing is believing.**
  2. **You only believe as much as you live.**
  3. **Faith is a blind leap into the unknown.**
- Discuss the following questions:
  1. **Why is it tough to step out in faith?**

2. What are some things that keep us from acting on our faith?

3. What are some situations in your life right now in which God is asking you to "live by faith, not by sight" (2 Corinthians 5:7)?

Being a person of faith...it's as easy as A-B-C!

I. Faith is being available.
  A. Faith is being open and available to whatever God wants to do. If you were to hear the voice of God in your life, would you be open and available to Him?
  B. Imagine if you were Mary or Joseph.
    1. Read Matthew 1:18-25. How did Joseph react to the angel's message?
      a. He accepted the direction as coming from God.
      b. He was open to doing God's will.
    2. Read Luke 1:26-38. What was Mary's reaction?
      a. She was troubled, yet open to hearing the message (v. 29).
      b. She questioned the validity of the message (v. 34).
      c. She made herself available, fulfilling God's purpose for her (v. 38).
II. Faith is believing.
  A. Faith is believing what God said and what He has promised to do.
    1. Read Luke 1:45. Elizabeth blessed Mary for believing God's message.
    2. In Matthew 1:24, Joseph trusted the message.
  B. Read Romans 4:21. It is knowing God will do what He promised.
  C. Read Hebrews 11:1. It is being sure of what you hope for and certain of what you don't see.
    1. Do you have the kind of faith that trusts so completely, you will believe what God says, even when it seems impossible (see Luke 1:37)?
    2. Do you see a way when there seems to be no way? That's radical faith!
    3. If you were to hear the voice of God in your life, would you believe?
III. Faith is committing to action and obedience.

A. Faith is more than being open—more than believing. Faith is committing to action.

   1. Mary and Joseph not only believed, but they also committed to obeying God and His plan. And not only did they believe it, but they also chose to live it out. Refer to Matthew 1:24 and Luke 1:38.

   2. Are you acting on what you believe? You only believe as much as you give.

B. Faith is more than talk—it's taking a step! Just like in the video clip. Is your faith one that takes action?

   1. It's one thing to say you believe—a truly radical faith moves you into action.

   2. Read James 2:17. Is your faith alive—or is it in need of a rescue call to 911? If you were to hear the voice of God in your life, would you obey and take action?

Small-Group Discussion

- If you have not already done so, divide students into small groups of five or six.
- Have students join their small groups.
- Give each student a copy of the Session One discussion questions from page 141 and a pen or pencil.
- Have students discuss the questions in their small groups.
- The questions in this first small group discussion time are geared toward helping students set goals for the retreat. Allow them some flexibility and help them set goals that are appropriate, challenging *and* attainable. Challenge students to allow Christ to work in their lives in such a way that they leave at the end of the weekend with their lives permanently changed.
- Close in prayer.

Session Two:
Faith at Work in Trials and Temptations

Objective

We all experience trials and temptations in our lives. Through faith in Christ, we have the tools necessary to meet and successfully conquer those trials and temptations. God uses trials within the life of the believer and we can choose to respond to those trials with an attitude of thankfulness, faith and trust.

Biblical Basis

Romans 8:28; Hebrews 10:23-25; James 1:1-12

Key Verses

"Consider it pure joy, my brothers, whenever you face trials of many kinds, because you know that the testing of your faith develops perserverance." James 1:2,3

Team Effort: What Would You Do?

- Divide group members into groups of five to eight.
- Have each group create a scenario that deals with an everyday trial or temptation that a teenager might face. You may want to give them some ideas of various scenarios, such as: your best friend suddenly begins to ignore you and starts telling everyone the secrets you shared with her; or a classmate threatens to beat you up because you will not allow him to copy your homework.
- After five to ten minutes, collect all the scenarios and redistribute them to the groups, so that each group doesn't get their own.
- Give each group another five to ten minutes to answer the question, "What would you do in this situation?"
- If there is time, have a few groups share their scenarios and what they would do in the midst of that trial or temptation.

In the Word: Faith in Adversity

I.   All of us go through tough times and trials in our lives—no one is exempt!
   A. Our attitude affects how we handle or how we react to tough times in our lives.
   B. We can respond by:
      1. **Escaping** them;
      2. **Explaining** them—asking why;
      3. **Exiting** them as soon as possible;
      4. **Enduring** them with the proper attitude.
   C. Refer back to the scenarios in the Team Effort and relate the four *Es* to some of the situations.

Read James 1:2-12, then explain: **Let's look at some ways to respond with a positive attitude toward trials.**

II. Three keys to having a good attitude, not a bad attitude.[1]
   A. Key One: Choose to have a joyful heart (see James 1:2-4).
      1. Trials will come into your life. It's not *if*, but *when* they will come.
      2. We can rejoice because:
         a. Trials are opportunities for growth in faith and trust;
         b. We know we will be stronger after the trial for future battles (see v. 4);
         c. We know that God is at work in our lives. He uses our trials to strengthen and mature us.
Discuss:
Why does God allow people to go through trials and tough times?
How does a person's relationship with God change as he or she goes through trials and problems?
How can you choose to have a joyful heart?
What would you tell a friend who is going through a trial right now?
   B. Key Two: Come to God for strength (see James 1:5-8).
      1. God will strengthen you when you ask Him to.

2. We need to ask continually for...

    a. Strength to continue under the trial.

    b. Wisdom not to miss opportunities within the trials.

    c. Perspective to see trials through His eyes.

Discuss:

What does verse 6 mean?

What effect does doubt have on a person when he or she prays?

When do you find it hardest to pray?

With what doubts have you struggled concerning God and prayer?

How can a person seek God for strength? Wisdom? Perspective?

    C. Key Three: Chase after the crown (see James 1:12).

      1. The key to making it through trials is to look at the finish line, the goal, the prize.

      2. If we keep our eyes on the goal, we will make it through trials with style.

      3. Focus your eyes on Jesus Christ and what He's doing in your life through the trial.

Discuss:

What reward waits for the person who perseveres under trials?

What is the goal that we should be focused on?

What takes our focus off the goal during trials?

How can we regain our focus in the midst of trials?

Application

- Explain: **Our quest to live faithfully through hard times isn't easy. Here are four anchors you can cling to in the midst of those trials and temptations:**

    Anchor 1:   Cling to Jesus in the midst of tough times.

    Anchor 2:   Cling to the fact that Jesus knows the outcome (see Romans 8:28).

    Anchor 3:   Cling to the support of those around you (see Hebrews 10:23-25).

    Anchor 4:   Cling to the lessons learned through the experience.

Small-Group Discussion

- Have students join their assigned small groups.
- Give each student a copy of the Session Two discussion questions on page 142 and a pen or pencil.
- Have students discuss the questions in their small groups.
- Close in prayer.

Session Three:
Faith at Work in Actions

Objective

To lead students to an understanding of how faith and works are inter-related and give them a true understanding that we are saved by faith, but assimilated into the Body of Christ by our works.

Biblical Basis

Luke 23:32-43; John 1:12; 3:16; Acts 16:31; 26:20; Romans 3:28; 10:9,10; Ephesians 2:8-10; Philippians 2:12,13; 1 Timothy 6:18; Hebrews 10:24,25; James 2:14-26; 1 John 3:16-18

Key Verses

"What good is it, my brothers, if a man claims to have faith but has no deeds? Can such faith save him?...faith by itself, if it is not accompanied by action, is dead." James 2:14,17

Team Effort Option 1: What Is Faith?

- Tell/read the following story:

  On June 30, 1858, Charles Blondin, arguably one of the best tightrope walkers of all time, stretched a tightrope across Niagara Falls. People came by train from Buffalo, New York, and Toronto, Canada, to see him walk across the tightrope that was suspended high above the raging falls.

As he stepped onto the tightrope, a hush fell over the crowd. He carried with him a 40-foot-long balance bar that weighed 39 pounds. When he finally stepped foot on the Canadian side, a huge cheer arose from the crowd. Then they began to shout in unison, "Blondin, Blondin, Blondin...." Finally Blondin held up his hand asking for the crowd's attention. He asked the crowd, "How many of you believe I can put someone on my shoulders and walk across?

First one person shouted, "I believe" and then a second and a third, until finally the whole crowd was shouting, "We believe! We believe! We believe!"

Then Blondin shouted, "Who would like to be that some-one?" All of a sudden everyone got quiet. They all said they believed, but no one was willing to risk their lives.

Blondin pointed his finger first at one person, then another and asked, "Would you like to get on my back as I go across?"

They all said, "No!" until he came to Mr. McDougle, his manager, who said, "Yes."

McDougle got on Blondin's back, and a deathly silence fell over the crowd as Blondin stepped out onto the tight rope. Carefully, step by step, Blondin made his way across....to safety on the other side.[2]

- Explain: **Faith is more than just believing in your mind, it means stepping out on that belief in action. Being a Christian means believing enough in Christ to climb on His back and go with Him no matter where He leads, even across Niagara Falls. If we fall into the trap of giving merit only to works and not to faith, we soon fall into legalism. Legalism means we do works for the sake of doing works, without faith. God wants us to have a living faith in Him that believes not only in thought but backs up belief by stepping out in action**
- Discuss the following questions:
  1. **According to the story, how would you define the word "faith"?**
  2. **What are some things that we have faith in?** (For example, that the car will work when you drive it; that a chair will support you when you sit in it.)

3. What does it mean to have faith in God?
4. Read James 2:14-17. What's the relationship between "faith" and "works" (actions)?

Team Effort Option 2: I Don't Have a Clue!

- Before the meeting, prepare three poster boards with one of the following words or phrases printed in large letters, one per sheet: "Agree," "Disagree" and "I don't have a clue!"
- Attach the three poster boards to three different walls or locations in the meeting room.
- After a leader reads each statement, students will move to the location in the room that best describes their feelings about the statement. Interact with a few people from each response group. The statements are as follows:

    1. We are saved by what we believe.
    2. We are saved by what we do.
    3. All we need to do to be saved is ask Jesus into our hearts.
    4. A person's walk with Jesus can be judged by the "fruit" their lives produce.

In the Word: True Faith

- In this study, students will be looking up several passages of Scripture dealing with the relationship between faith and works.
- Ask students to look up the passages, asking them to read it in light of the question, **What does this have to say about faith and works?**
- Let your students wrestle a little bit with the issue. Be ready to play "devil's advocate" with the group.
- **Option:** If your group size allows for it, you may want to divide the whole group into three smaller groups, assigning one of the following sections to each group. Give each group the verses to look up and the questions they need to answer. Have the groups come back together and share their main point, the verses and the answers to the questions. Allow the other small-groups' members to have input to the questions as well.
I. True Faith Leads to Salvation.
   A. Read the following passages: Luke 23:32-43; John 1:12; 3:16; Acts 16:31; Romans 3:28; 10:9,10; Ephesians 2:8-10.

B. We are saved by faith and faith alone.

C. There is nothing we do to *earn* our salvation. It is a gift from God!

Discuss:

How is a person saved?

Why do people need to be saved?

Why is it difficult to share the message of Christ with others?

II. True Faith Leads to a Lifestyle Change.

    A. Read the following passages: Acts 26:20; Philippians 2:12,13; James 2:14-26.

    B. True faith will lead to a life that is transformed (different, changed).

    C. True faith is not a "fire insurance" policy but a surrendering of your life to Jesus Christ. There *will be* change!

Discuss:

What is destructive about having faith without works or a changed lifestyle?

How is being Christians supposed to change the way we live?

What are some areas in your life that you need God to help you change/work on?

III. True Faith Leads to Action.

    A. Read the following passages: 1 Timothy 6:18; Hebrews 10:24,25; 1 John 3:16-18.

    B. True faith will lead to living out our faith in the real world.

    C. We obey, not to be saved, but because of being saved and the incredible things God has done for each of us.

Discuss:

What are some ways we as Christians can live out our faith in action?

How can living out our faith in action show the world who Jesus is?

What action do you need to take in living out your faith?

Application

- Explain: **In the life of a Christian, faith and works must both be evident. What happens when we err on either side of the faith/works relationship? For instance, what happens if we are so busy doing good works in God's name that we don't know Him personally?**

Small-Group Discussion

- Have students join their assigned small groups.
- Give each student a copy of the Session Three discussion questions on page 143 and a pen or pencil.
- Have students discuss the questions in their small groups.
- Close in prayer.

Session Four: Faith at Work in Relationships

Objective

Faith not only helps us live in right relationships with God, but it also helps us to live in right relationships with each other. Living by faith in Christ betters our relationships with each other.

Biblical Basis

Matthew 12:34,35; James 3:1-18

Key Verse

"For out of the overflow of the heart the mouth speaks. The good man brings good things out of the good stored up in him, and the evil man brings evil things out of the evil stored up in him." Matthew 12:34,35

Team Effort: Show Me the Way

- Before the meeting, set up an obstacle course using chairs, tables, podium, eggs, etc.
- Place the members of the group in various locations at the front of the room.
- Select one volunteer from the group and blindfold him or her. Explain that he or she is going to be directed through the obstacle

course by the whole group. The rest of the group will be giving the blindfolded person instructions on how to get through it.

- Spin the person around a few times and send him or her through the obstacle course. Invariably at the beginning the volunteer will get confused by all the shouting, but will then hone in on one voice and listen to that person's directions. At the end of the experience, discuss the following questions:

    1. (To the volunteer) **What was it like to get through the course?**
    2. (To the volunteer) **Why was it confusing at the beginning?**
    3. (To the volunteer) **What did you do to get through the course?**
    4. (To the group) **How is this experience like walking by faith in real life?**

In the Word: Faith at Work in Relationships

- Explain: **Part of living out our faith in Christ is living it out with others in relationships. We need each other, yet one of the biggest roadblocks in our relationships with others is our words. What we say to each other matters a great deal. Our words can be as soothing as a cool breeze or as fiery as a blazing fire. What comes from our mouths affects not only others but ourselves as well. In our relationships with one another we have to choose: Will we use our words to build up or to tear down? One of the most essential ingredients in living out our faith in Christ through relationships is what we say to one another. Let's look at what James has to say.**

- Read James 3:1-12. Then explain: **James challenged us to use our words to build up others. He also showed us what that looks like in relationships.**

- Read James 3:13-18. After reading the passage, explain: **There is no room for envy, jealousy or arrogance in the life of a Christian. When we esteem ourselves higher than those around us, we are sure to have broken and hurtful relationships. Let's take a look at how James speaks to us about how to live out our faith in Christ through our relationships.**

Application

- Read Matthew 12:34,35. Remind students that the words that

come out of their mouths come from their hearts. Challenge them to examine their heart attitudes.

- James 3:17 lists the following as marks of a "good heart":

Pure	Merciful
Peace-loving	Fruitful
Considerate	Impartial
Submissive	Sincere

So what does it look like in real life? It starts with a choice. Here are four action steps.

Action Step 1: **Choose to put the needs of others before your own.**
Action Step 2: **Choose to accept others' differences.**
Action Step 3: **Choose to encourage others in all ways.**
Action Step 4: **Choose to pray for those who are difficult.**

Small-Group Discussion

- Have students join their assigned small groups.
- Give each student a copy of the Session Four discussion questions on page 144 and a pen or pencil.
- Have students discuss the questions in their small groups.
- Close in prayer.

Debriefing Session

- Have a time for students to reflect on the weekend and what they learned. This can be done just before you leave the retreat or when you return home. If you wait to debrief upon your return, do it before students leave for their homes.
- See page 12 in the Retreat Guidelines section for debriefing session ideas.

Notes
1. Jim Burns, gen. ed. and Mike DeVries, comp., *Bible Study Outlines and Messages* (Ventura, CA: Gospel Light, 1998), pp. 226-227.
2. Jim Burns, gen. ed. and Greg McKinnon, comp., *Illustrations, Stories and Quotes to Hang Your Message On* (Ventura, CA: Gospel Light, 1997), pp. 115-116.

Session One:
Discussion Starters

1. Why did you come on the retreat this weekend?

2. What are a few of your expectations?

    What do you want to get out of this weekend?

3. Read Matthew 20:29-34. If Jesus were to ask you, "What do you want me to do for you?" what would you say?

4. Read together Hebrews 11:1. When you think of the word "faith," what comes to mind?

    How would you define the word "faith" to someone?

Session Two:
Discussion Starters

1. What do you think God is trying to teach you through the current trials and situations you are facing?

2. In what areas do you need to ask God for His wisdom?

3. What temptations do you need God's help to resist?

4. What are some steps you will take the next time you find yourself in the midst of either a trial or temptation?

Session Three: Discussion Starters

1. Can true faith exist without works? Explain.

2. Can godly works exist without true faith? Explain.

3. What's the relationship between faith and works?

4. What does James mean by the statement "faith without deeds is dead" (James 2:26)?

5. What works in your life are evidence of your faith?

Session Four:
Discussion Starters

1. What are some ways our words can tear down or hurt others?

2. What are some ways our words can build up others?

3. What does James teach about how we should use our tongues?

4. What does James teach about envy and selfishness?

5. What can you do in the next week to live out your faith in the words you speak to others?

Knowing Who We Serve

The Big Idea

We often serve in church without having an understanding of who we are serving. We think we are serving the social concerns of our day or serving others when in actuality the One we are serving is the almighty, all-knowing, ever-present God.

Key Verse

"Serve wholeheartedly, as if you were serving the Lord, not men." Ephesians 6:7

Aims

During this retreat, you will guide students to:
- Examine their knowledge of God;
- Discover truths about who God is;
- Implement a plan for getting to know God in a more intimate way.

Location

A group campsite or retreat center, one to two and a half hours away

Time Frame

Friday night through Sunday night

Budget

$15 to $30 per student, depending on facility

Memory Verses

Psalm 14:2; Jeremiah 23:23,24; Matthew 28:18; Luke 24:45

Advance Preparation

❏ Organize student leadership teams at least one month before the retreat. Assign an adult leader to oversee each team. See the Retreat Guidelines section on page 11 for suggestions. Suggested teams for this retreat include:
  - Bon Appetit Team
  - Equipment Team
  - Transportation Team
  - Focus Team

❏ About a month before the retreat, give students the list of memory verses to begin to memorize.

❏ Set up small JAM Session groups (five to six students per group) and assign each group an adult leader to facilitate discussions.

❏ Contact retreat facility to check for availability of electrical outlets.

❏ Obtain white board or poster board (or overhead projector, transparency and screen if electric plugs are available) and appropriate writing instruments.

❏ Borrow or rent tents, cooking equipment and trailer(s) to haul equipment if you are camping out.

❏ Collect firewood for campfires.

❏ Photocopy student pages 161-170.

❏ Prepare questions and buy prizes for "Warm-Up: I Know!" (p. 154).

❏ Collect recreation equipment needed for planned (and unplanned) activities, i.e., frisbees, volleyballs, softballs, bats and mitts, etc.

❏ Obtain signed medical and liability release forms from each retreat participant.

❏ Meet with leaders to finalize retreat schedule.

❏

❏

❏

What Leaders Need to Bring

- ❏ Paper and pens/pencils
- ❏ Colored 3x5-inch index cards (needed if using them in session 1 "Things to Think About" section)
- ❏ White board, poster board or overhead projector, transparencies, extension cord and appropriate writing instruments
- ❏ Firewood for campfires
- ❏ Photocopies of all student pages
- ❏ Sporting equipment for activities
- ❏ Signed copies of medical and liability release forms
- ❏
- ❏
- ❏

What Students Need to Bring

- ❏ Sleeping bag and pillow
- ❏ Air mattress or foam pad (if camping out)
- ❏ Appropriate clothing
- ❏ One duffel bag for clothing and toiletries
- ❏ One backpack with notebook, Bible, journal, pens or pencils and wallet
- ❏ Appetite and smiles
- ❏ Folding beach chair, blanket or towel for campfire meetings
- ❏ Sack dinner for Friday night
- ❏ $40.00 cash in small bills—ones and fives
- ❏ Medical and liability release forms
- ❏ Personal sporting equipment, i.e., mitts/gloves, frisbees, etc.
- ❏
- ❏
- ❏

Retreat Schedule

Friday

4:00 P.M.	Meet at church, register and load up vehicles (Transportation and Equipment Team)
5:00 P.M.	Leave for mountains; eat en route
7:30 P.M.	Arrive at campsite/set up
8:00 P.M.	JAM Session One (Focus Team)
8:30 P.M.	Evening worship/prayer by the campfire
9:15 P.M.	Campfire s'mores (Bon Appetit Team)
10:00 P.M.	Tent/cabin time—bedtime

Saturday

7:00 A.M.	Wake up and personal devotions
8:00 A.M.	Breakfast (Bon Appetit Team)
9:00 A.M.	Session One: God *Is* Everywhere—Always!
10:00 A.M.	JAM Session Two (Focus Team)
10:30 A.M.	Free time until lunch*
12:00 P.M.	Lunch (Bon Appetit Team)
1:00 P.M.	Session Two: God Is All-Knowing
2:00 P.M.	JAM Session Three (Focus Team)
2:30 P.M.	Free time until dinner*
5:30 P.M.	Return to campsite or cabins
6:00 P.M.	Dinner (Bon Appetit Team)
7:00 P.M.	Session Three: God Is All-Powerful
8:00 P.M.	JAM Session Four (Focus Team)
8:30 P.M.	Worship around the campfire
9:00 P.M.	Snack time (Bon Appetit Team)
10:00 P.M.	Tent/cabin time—bedtime

Sunday

7:00 A.M.	Wake up and personal devotionals
8:00 A.M.	Breakfast (Bon Appetit Team)
9:00 A.M.	Worship and praise
9:30 A.M.	Session Four: God Is Knowable
10:30 A.M.	JAM Session Five (Focus Team)

11:00 A.M.	Free time until lunch*
1:00 P.M.	Lunch (Bon Appetit Team)
2:00 P.M.	Pack up and load vehicles
3:00 P.M.	Leave for church
6:00 P.M.	Arrive at church

*Free Time Suggestions: Too much unstructured free time can lead to mischief or other problems. As a part of free times, be sure to plan some all-group activities, such as hiking, volleyball, softball or any other organized recreation. You can also add creative activities and games: some simply fun activities, some that will build community, or some that will even teach a point. These activities and games are great for adding a sense of fun and adventure while building some great memories and group camaraderie. See the Retreat Guidelines section on page 14 for great resources to aid you in planning activities and games.

The Plan

Knowing Who We Serve

JAM Session One

- Gather everyone around the campfire or in the meeting area.
- If you have not done so before leaving for the retreat, assign students to their JAM Session Groups. They will return to their assigned groups throughout the retreat.
- Have students join their assigned JAM Session groups.
- Hand out JAM Session One questions on page 161. Have the groups discuss the questions.
- When groups have finished discussing questions, have worship leaders lead a few songs about God around the campfire.

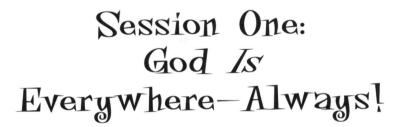

Objective

During this session you will guide students to:
- Examine the Bible to understand God's presence;
- Discover that God is everywhere at the same time;
- Implement what God's presence means in our lives.

Biblical Basis

Job 34:21,22; Psalm 139:7-12; Jeremiah 23:23,24; John 4:24

Key Verses

"'Am I only a God nearby,' declares the LORD, 'and not a God far away? Can anyone hide in secret places so that I cannot see him?' declares the LORD. 'Do not I fill heaven and earth?' declares the LORD." Jeremiah 23:23,24

Warm-Up: Sardines

- Choose one person to be "It." That person hides and after a few minutes everyone goes to find him or her. The object of the game is that when they find the person who is *It*, they are to hide with that person. This continues until the last person finds the "Can of Sardines."

> **Note:** If this is done in an outdoor setting, set boundaries beforehand so you don't permanently lose someone!

- Play the game as long as you want, but quit before students lose interest. When you are ready to make the transition, explain: **We are going to study about where God is. Sometimes we think that we can hide from God or hide things from God. Let's begin to understand who God is by understanding where He is.**

> **BIG IDEA** God has always been and always will be everywhere at the same time—eternal and omnipresent.

Team Effort

- Brainstorm with the whole group: **If you could be everywhere at the same time, where would you most like to be? Where would you least like to be?**

In the Word: Understanding God's Presence

- Read Psalm 139:7-12 and Jeremiah 23:23,24, then ask students: **According to these verses, where are some of the places that God is?**
- Read Job 34:21,22. Discuss the following:
  How should this verse affect our thinking when we have trials, tribulations and temptations?
  How can God occupy all space at the same time? Read John 4:24.

Things to Think About

- Hand out paper and pens or pencils for students to write their reponses (or 3x5-inch cards for item 3), or have them write their responses in their notebooks or journals. Choose *one* of the following activities to have them respond to:
1. **You have five minutes to write a letter to God sharing how thankful you are that He is always near.**
2. **List situations where you have felt lonely and write next to each incident: "But God, You were there!"**
3. Give each student a 3x5-inch card. **On this card, write: "God is everywhere!" and put it in your pocket or Bible to remind you of His presence.**

JAM Session Two

- Have students join their assigned JAM Session groups.
- Hand out JAM Session Two questions on page 162. Have the groups discuss the questions.
- When the session is over, have them get on their knees and thank God for always being near. Encourage the students to continue to think about God during their free time.

Session Two:
God Is All-Knowing

Objectives

During this session, you will guide students to:
- Examine the knowledge of God;
- Discover that God knows the future and our thoughts;
- Implement a lifestyle of seeking after the knowledge of God by spending time with Him.

Biblical Basis

2 Kings 19:25; Psalm 94:11; 139:1,16; Isaiah 55:8,9; Jeremiah 29:11; Matthew 12:25; Luke 12:4-7; Romans 8:28,31; Philippians 4:13; James 1:5

Key Verse

"If any of you lacks wisdom, he should ask God, who gives generously to all without finding fault, and it will be given to him." James 1:5

Warm-Up: I Know!

- Make a list of things that you think students may or may not know something about. Make sure that *you* know the correct answers.

    Sample question: What is a hostel?
    Answer: A place of supervised lodging for young people

- Ask students who think they know the right answer to respond by standing up with both arms in the air. Choose one student at a time to tell the answer.
- When a student answers the question correctly, give him or her a prize, such as a candy bar, a soda, etc.

Team Effort: Brainstorming

- Explain: **We are going to brainstorm some questions that we'd like to ask God. For example, I would like to ask God who my**

children are going to marry. We'll write your questions on the white board (or poster board or overhead).

- Allow 10 minutes for the students to share some funny and not so funny things that they wish they could know. Then explain: **God knows about all of this. He knows the future and our thoughts,** *and* **He knows us. Let's study about some of the things that God knows.**

God knows all things, the future, our thoughts and all about us. When you need help, ask Him for wisdom and knowledge. **BIG IDEA**

In the Word: Trying to Understand What God Knows

- Read the following verses and discuss what the verses tell about what God knows.
  - I. God knows the future.
      - A. 2 Kings 19:25—He has a plan.
      - B. Psalm 139:16—He planned your days before you were born.
      - C. Jeremiah 29:11—His plan is for our good.
  - II. God knows your thoughts.
      - A. Psalm 94:11; 139:1-4—He knows our thoughts before we think them.
      - B. Isaiah 55:8,9—His thoughts and ways are different than ours.
      - C. Matthew 12:25—Jesus knew the thoughts of those around Him.
  - III. God even knows you and cares for you.
      - • Luke 12:4-7—He even knows the number of hairs on your head!
  - IV. Ask God for special wisdom if you need it.
      - • James 1:5—Tap into the source!

Things to Think About: Get to Know God and Get to Know All Things

- Explain: **If we truly want to understand all things, we need to know the One who knows all things. Consider how much time you spend getting to know God. Spend some time in your** prayer journal asking God for help to understand Him and His ways!

- Ask students to respond by writing their answers to the following in their journals:
  1. **What are two things for which you need special wisdom from God?**
  2. **Since we know that God knows our future plans (see Jeremiah 29:11), how can we rest assured that He will not give us anything that we cannot handle?** (Also see Romans 8:28,31; Philippians 4:13.)

JAM SESSION THREE

- Have students join their assigned JAM Session groups.
- Hand out JAM Session Three questions on page 163 and pens or pencils.
- Have the groups discuss the questions.

Session Three: God Is All-Powerful

Objectives

During this session, you will guide students to:
- Examine the power of God;
- Discover that God has the power over all;
- Implement a renewed focus and trust in God's control.

Biblical Basis

Genesis 1; Exodus 14:21,22; Job 2:1-10; Psalm 119; Jeremiah 29:11; Matthew 6:25-34; 28:1-10,18; Mark 1:27; John 6:8-14; 11; Romans 13:1-5

Key Verse

"Then Jesus came to them and said, 'All authority in heaven and on earth has been given to me.'" Matthew 28:18

Warm-Up: Power Rate

- Hand out the "Power Rate" chart (p. 166) and pens and pencils to students.
- Have students complete the chart, then discuss their answers.

Team Effort: You Have the Power!

- Ask students: **If you had all the power in the world to do whatever you wanted, what are the top three things you would do?**
- Choose a student to write the group's responses on a white board or a sheet of poster board.

> Their reponses will give you insight into what the students are truly concerned about. Have an adult leader write down their responses for use for future Bible study, meeting or retreat ideas.

> God has power and control over all things! **BIG IDEA**

In the Word: The Power and Control of God

- Explain: **God has control over everything. God has control over Satan, death, countries, authorities, nature and life.**
- Read Job 2:1-10. Discuss God's power over Satan, then ask: **What restrictions did God put on Satan?**
- Read Mark 1:27. Discuss who Jesus had power over, then discuss the following:
  1. **What does Romans 13:1-5 have to say about God's control over the world's governments?**
  2. **What does Exodus 14:21,22 and John 6:8-14 say about who is in control over nature?**
  3. **How does the creation of the world** (see Genesis 1) **and Jesus' resurrection** (see Matthew 28:1-10) **prove God's control over life?**

Things to Think About: Don't Worry, God's in Control

Read Matthew 6:25-34; then ask: **How does Jesus assure us that God is in control and He will take care of us?**

Read Jeremiah 29:11; then explain: **God has great plans for each of you. You need to keep your focus on Him and not on the things of the world.** Give students 10 minutes to talk to God in their prayer journals about all that they have learned during this session.

SMALL GROUP

JAM Session Four

- Have students join their assigned JAM Session groups.
- Hand out JAM Session Four questions on page 164. Have the groups discuss the questions.
- Close the session by asking students to spend 10 minutes writing in their journals in response to the last question.

Session Four: God Is Knowable

Objectives

During this session, you will guide students to:
- Examine ways that spiritual things can relate to their world;
- Discover three ways to better understand God;
- Implement a plan for seeking after God.

Biblical Basis

Joshua 1:8; Psalm 119; 139:23; 143:5; Proverbs 2:1-6; Romans 1:28; Ephesians 3:20; 1 John 5:14

Key Verse

"The Lord looks down from heaven on the sons of men to see if there are any who understand, any who seek God." Psalm 14:2

Team Effort: Finish the Thought

- Hand out copies of "Team Effort: Finish the Thought" (p. 167). Give each student a pen or pencil.
- Have students pair up and give them five minutes to complete as many sentences as possible.
- Have students share some of their responses.

We need to spend time and energy seeking after God. BIG IDEA

In the Word: Ways to Get to Know and Understand God

- Divide students into their JAM Session groups to read and discuss Psalm 119.
- Have them read the psalm, assigning 5 to 10 verses per person, depending on the size of the groups.

Be sensitive to students who may be poor readers. Allow students to opt out of reading aloud if they don't "feel" like reading. Just make sure you have assigned some readers to each group!

- Hand out copies of the discussion questions "Ways to Get to Know and Understand God" (p. 169); then have them discuss the questions in their small groups.

Things to Think About: The Consequences of Not Searching After God

- Give each student a copy of the handout "The Consequences of Not Searching After God" (p. 170) and a pen or pencil.
- Read Romans 1:28 and discuss question 1. Then have them complete parts 2 and 3 on their own.

JAM SESSION FIVE

- Have students rejoin their assigned JAM Session groups.
- Hand out JAM Session Five questions on page 165. Have the groups discuss the questions.
- Close the session by challenging students to commit to reading God's Word regularly in order to understand God in a deeper way over the next year. Share the following illustration of an owner's manual:

> **When you buy something new, you need to read the owner's manual in order to understand how it works. If you never read our owner's manual—God's Word—you will never fully understand how to live the Christian life.**

Debriefing Session

- Have a time for students to reflect on the weekend and what they learned. This can be done just before you leave the retreat or when you return home. If you wait to debrief upon your return, do it before students leave for their homes.
- See page 12 in the Retreat Guidelines section for debriefing session ideas.

JAM Session One

Discuss the following questions and write down your answers:

1. Write down one memory verse for the weekend.

2. Please list 5 to 10 things that you know about God.

3. On a scale of 1 to 10 (10 means I really know God), how would you rate yourself?

JAM Session Two

Discuss the following questions and write down your answers:

1. What are three things that you learned about God in this session? Write a verse reference that relates to each item you list.

2. What does the fact that God is everywhere at the same time mean to you?

3. How does the fact of God's omnipresence affect the way you should act?

4. Can we pray to God anytime we want? Do you think that He can always hear you? Why?

5. Can we call on His help and know that He is near us? Explain.

6. Why does God allow us to go through tough times?

   Since He is always near us, why doesn't He make life easy?

   Fill in the blank: "Hard times make us _____."

JAM Session Three

Please consider the following questions and write down your answers:

1. What would it be like if you could know everything?

2. What kinds of bad things could people do if they knew everything?

   What good things could they do?

3. We can be so glad that God is faithful and trustworthy to have such knowledge. He uses it for good. Read Romans 8:28. How does it affect you to know that God intends the best for your life?

4. Read Jeremiah 29:11. Do you really believe that God knows what is best for your life? Are you trusting Him? Take 10 minutes alone with God. Write in your prayer journal 10 things in your life that you thank God for.

JAM Session Four

Discuss the following questions and write down your answers:

1. List 20 things in *your* life over which God has power.

2. List other things in the world around us that God has control over. Work together as a group to write a verse reference next to each item.

3. Many people want to be a friend to someone who is powerful. Our study helps us understand that God is all powerful. There is none that is more powerful than God. How can you nurture your relationship with God? Read Psalm 119 together.

4. In your journal, write down one step you will take to improve your relationship with God. Spend time in prayer asking God to reveal what He wants you to do.

JAM Session Five

Discuss the following questions and write down your answers:

1. What are three things that you can do to better understand the God that you serve?

2. On a scale of 1 to 10 (10 means I really know God), how would you rate yourself?

3. What are the three attributes of God that we learned about this weekend?

4. In your journal write your memory verses for the weekend.

5. Also write what God has been teaching you during this weekend. What change do you need to make in your life in response to what you have learned?

Power Rate

The following list consists of things that are considered to be related to power. Rate them on a scale of 1 to 10 (1 being weak and 10 being way powerful!). Circle the number that expresses your answer.

	The weakest									Way powerful!
Nature	1	2	3	4	5	6	7	8	9	10
Satan	1	2	3	4	5	6	7	8	9	10
Water	1	2	3	4	5	6	7	8	9	10
A volcano	1	2	3	4	5	6	7	8	9	10
The Mafia	1	2	3	4	5	6	7	8	9	10
The F.B.I.	1	2	3	4	5	6	7	8	9	10
A bean burrito	1	2	3	4	5	6	7	8	9	10
The U.S. president	1	2	3	4	5	6	7	8	9	10
Demons	1	2	3	4	5	6	7	8	9	10
A nuclear missile	1	2	3	4	5	6	7	8	9	10
Illegal drugs	1	2	3	4	5	6	7	8	9	10
My parents	1	2	3	4	5	6	7	8	9	10
The government	1	2	3	4	5	6	7	8	9	10
The C.I.A.	1	2	3	4	5	6	7	8	9	10

Team Effort:
Finish the Thought

Work together to complete the sentences with the appropriate words.

Examples:
God's Word is like *a good book: If you don't read it, it is worthless.*
Prayer is like *a telephone: If you don't answer or dial out, you will never talk to your friend.*
Meditation is like *a good rain: Once it starts, it turns into a river of thought.*
God is like *the internet: He is everywhere.*

The Bible is like _____.

The Bible is like _____.

The Bible is like _____.

The Bible is like _____.

Prayer is like _____.

Prayer is like _____.

Prayer is like _____.

Prayer is like _____.

Meditation is like _____.

Meditation is like _____.

Meditation is like _____.

Meditation is like _____.

God is like _____.

God is like _____.

God is like _____.

God is like _____.

In the Word:
Ways to Get to Know and
Understand God

Read Psalm 119, then discuss the following questions:

1. Why is studying the Word of God important to understanding God?

2. What does Proverbs 2:1-6 say about trying to understand and know God?

3. When we pray we can ask God to help us understand His ways. How could the following verses apply to you?
   Psalm 139:23

   Ephesians 3:20

   1 John 5:14

4. According to the following verses, why is meditation on God's Word important?
   Joshua 1:8

   Psalm 119:27

   Psalm 119:97

   Psalm 119:99

   Psalm 143:5

Things to Think About: The Consequences of Not Searching After God

Read Romans 1:28 and discuss the following:

1. How is this happening today?

2. Do you think people want to understand God today?
   Why or why not?

   What is the evidence?

3. Set personal goals for yourself in the areas of Bible study, prayer and meditation by placing a check mark beside each action you will take:
   In daily Bible study I will read...
   ❑ One verse.
   ❑ One chapter.
   ❑ One book.
   ❑ Other _____.

   I will pray...
   ❑ At all three meals.
   ❑ When I wake up and when I go to bed.
   ❑ Other _____.

   I will meditate on Scripture by...
   ❑ Reading the verse in my pocket.
   ❑ Memorizing one verse a week.
   ❑ Setting my watch to beep every hour and repeat the verse I am learning.
   ❑ Other: _____.

   Other ways I will seek God:

Scripture Index

Old Testament

GENESIS

1	156
1:26,31	113
2:18-25	113,120
6:9 - 8:11	52
12:1-10	52
13:1,2	52
39	52

EXODUS

14:21,22	156
20:14	113, 120

DEUTERONOMY

6:14,15	95

JOSHUA

1:8	27,158,169
4:1-7	39
24:24	99

JUDGES

4:1-16	52

2 SAMUEL

22:1-8	31,44

2 KINGS

19:25	154

JOB

2:1-10	156
34:21,22	152

PSALMS

14:2	146,158
42:4	45
66:18-20	95
69:30	45
94:11	154
100:4	45
119	156,158,164,169
119:11	95
139:1,16	154
139:7-12	152
139:23	158,169
143:5	158,169
150	121

PROVERBS

2:1-6	158,169
21:13	95

ECCLESIASTES

8:7,8	52

ISAIAH

55:8,9	154

JEREMIAH

23:23,24	146,152
29:11	154,156,163

EZEKIEL

14:7,8	95

AMOS

5:14	95

New Testament

Page numbers in **boldface** type indicate Key Verse for each retreat.

5:19,20	113
6:9	99

EPHESIANS

2:8-10	134
3:20	158,169
4:32	95
5:1,3	117
5:3-5	115
5:4	45
6:7,8	99,**145**

PHILIPPIANS

1:1-11	73,82
2:1-5,14,15	75,83
2:3,4	113
2:12,13	134
3:1-16	84
3:12-14	77
3:17-4:1	52
4:4-13	79,85
4:6	**45**,86,95,102
4:13	154

1 THESSALONIANS

4:1-8	115,117
4:3	115
4:13-18	56
5:1-6	59

1 TIMOTHY

6:18	134

HEBREWS

10:23-25	131
10:24,25	56,134
11:1	**127**,141
11:7-9	52
12:1,2	77,84
13:4	113

JAMES

1:1-12	131
1:2,3	131
1:5	154
2:14-26	134
2:17	127
2:24	**122**
2:26	143
3:1-18	138
4:3	95
4:13-15	52

1 PETER

1:18,19	35
2:4-8	27
2:11	117
2:12	99
2:21-25	35
3:18	35
4:10	99

2 PETER

3:1-14	56
3:10-13	59

1 JOHN

1:8—2:1	95
3:2,3	59
3:16-18	134
5:11,12	52
5:14	158,169

JUDE

14-24	56

REVELATION

3:2,3	59
4:1-8	59
21:1-7	59
22:7,12,20	59

Page numbers in **boldface** type indicate Key Verse for each retreat.

Add a New Member to Your Youth Staff.

Jim Burns is president of the National Institute of Youth Ministry.

Meet Jim Burns. He won't play guitar and he doesn't do windows, but he will take care of your programming needs. That's because his new curriculum, **YouthBuilders Group Bible Studies,** is a comprehensive program designed to take your group through their high school years. (If you have junior high kids in your group, **YouthBuilders** works for them too.)

For less than $6 a month, you'll get Jim Burns' special recipe of high-involvement, discussion-oriented, Bible-centered studies. It's the next generation of Bible curriculum for youth—and with Jim on your staff, you'll be free to spend more time one-on-one with the kids in your group.

Here are some of Youth-Builders' hottest features:

- Reproducible pages—one book fits your whole group
- Wide appeal—big groups, small groups—even adjusts to combine junior high/high school groups
- Hits home—special section to involve parents with every session of the study
- Interactive Bible discovery—geared to help young people find answers themselves
- Cheat sheets—a Bible *Tuck-In*™ with all the session information on a single page
- Flexible format—perfect for Sunday mornings, midweek youth meetings, or camps and retreats
- Three studies in one—each study has three four-session modules that examine critical life choices.

   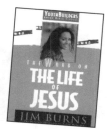

12 Books in the Series!

The Word on Sex, Drugs & Rock 'N' Roll
ISBN 08307.16424 $16.99

The Word on Prayer and the Devotional Life
ISBN 08307.16432 $16.99

The Word on the Basics of Christianity
ISBN 08307.16440 $16.99

The Word on Being a Leader, Serving Others & Sharing Your Faith
ISBN 08307.16459 $16.99

The Word on Helping Friends in Crisis
ISBN 08307.16467 $16.99

The Word on the Life of Jesus
ISBN 08307.16475 $16.99

The Word on Finding and Using Your Spiritual Gifts
ISBN 08307.17897 $16.99

The Word on the Sermon on the Mount
ISBN 08307.17234 $16.99

The Word on Spiritual Warfare
ISBN 08307.17242 $16.99

The Word on the New Testament
ISBN 08307.17250 $16.99

The Word on the Old Testament
ISBN 08307.17269 $16.99

The Word on Family
ISBN 08307.17277 $16.99

More Great Resources from Jim Burns

Drugproof Your Kids
Stephen Arterburn and Jim Burns
Solid biblical principles are combined with the most effective prevention and intervention techniques to give parents a guide they can trust.
ISBN 08307.17714 $10.99

Drugproof Your Kids Video
A 90-minute seminar featuring Stephen Arterburn and Jim Burns. Includes a reproducible syllabus.
SPCN 85116.00876 $19.99

Parenting Teens Positively Video *Featuring Jim Burns*
Understand the forces shaping the world of a teenager and what you can do to be a positive influence. This powerful message of hope is for anyone working with—or living with—youth. Includes reproducible syllabus. UPC 607135.000655 $29.99

Surviving Adolescence
Jim Burns
Jim Burns helps teens—and their parents—negotiate the path from adolescence to adulthood with real-life stories that show how to make it through the teen years in one piece. ISBN 08307.20650 $9.99

For these and more great resources and to learn about NIYM's leadership training, call **1-800-397-9725.**

Gospel Light

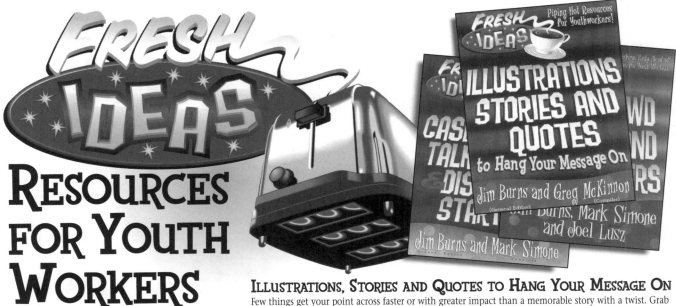

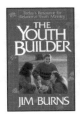

What in the world is *NIYM?*

A.) The Neurotically Inclined Yo-Yo Masters
B.) The Neatest Incidental Yearbook Mystery
C.) The Natural Ignition Yields of Marshmallows
D.) The National Institute of Youth Ministry

If you deliberately picked A, B, or C you're the reason Jim Burns started NIYM! If you picked D, you can go to the next page. In any case, you could learn more about NIYM. Here are some IQ score-raisers:

Jim Burns started NIYM to:
• Meet the growing needs of training and equipping youth workers and parents
• Develop excellent resources and events for young people—in the U.S. and internationally
• Empower young people and their families to make wise decisions and experience a vital Christian lifestyle.

NIYM can make a difference in your life and enhance your youth work skills through these special events:

Institutes—These consist of week-long, in-depth small-group training sessions for youth workers.

Trainer of Trainees—NIYM will train you to train others. You can use this training with your volunteers, parents and denominational events. You can go through the certification process and become an official NIYM associate. (No, you don't get a badge or decoder ring).

International Training—Join NIYM associates to bring youth ministry to kids and adults around the world. (You'll learn meanings to universal words like "yo!" and "hey!")

Custom Training—These are special training events for denominational groups, churches, networks, colleges and seminaries.

Parent Forums—We'll come to your church or community with two incredible hours of learning, interaction and fellowship. It'll be fun finding out who makes your kids tick!

Youth Events—Dynamic speakers, interaction and drama bring a powerful message to kids through a fun and fast-paced day. Our youth events include: This Side Up, Radical Respect, Surviving Adolescence and Peer Leadership.

For brain food or a free information packet about the National Institute of Youth Ministry, write to:

NIYM
P.O. Box 4374 • San Clemente, CA 92674
Tel: (714) 498-4418 • Fax: (714) 498-0037 • NIYMin@aol.com